John Kuada
Olav Jull Sørensen

Internationalization of Companies from Developing Countries

Pre-publication
REVIEWS,
COMMENTARIES,
EVALUATIONS . . .

"**T**his book tackles a very relevant issue within today's globalization context. It reviews the conceptual framework for developing country firm entry and performance in the international market, applies these concepts to a case country, Ghana, and then takes a critical look at the conceptual framework and suggests ways and means of adjustment. The analysis of the conceptual framework is sound, the choice of the case country is opportune, and the critical reassessment of the theoretical base, in light of the empirical evidence, is effective. What is especially innovative in the text are the developing country contexts and the discussion of these countries' firm internationalization policies and strategies, with a focus on the specific requirements of the countries."

M. S. S. El-Namaki, PhD
Dean and Director of Maastricht School of Management,
The Netherlands

More pre-publication
REVIEWS, COMMENTARIES, EVALUATIONS . . .

"*Internationalization of Companies from Developing Countries* reviews and critiques existing theories of economic development and finds them to be either biased by perspectives from the more economically developed world or simply wrong. Using the top twenty exporting companies in Ghana as a case study, the authors demonstrate some of the key features that make Western models of development and marketing inappropriate in Sub-Saharan Africa. Chief among these are the differing models of management practices in Ghana, including companies that rely on humane care for the extended family and social embeddedness in business dealings generally. Furthermore, the historical and cultural conditions that applied during the economic development of the West and of certain parts of Asia do not apply in sub-Saharan Africa, creating further problems for existing models of economic development.

The book makes its strongest contribution to the literature on development by suggesting development principles specific to Ghana and African countries with similar cultural and historical backgrounds. It adds upstream internationalization to the more common model of downstream internationalization, for example. These insights derive from an empirical survey of the most active exporting nations in Ghana. Anyone dealing with economic development in the less affluent world will find this a useful book. Those working in Sub-Saharan Africa will find it especially enriching."

Russell W. Belk, PhD
N. Eldon Tanner Professor,
David Eccles School of Business,
University of Utah,
Salt Lake City

International Business Press®
An Imprint of The Haworth Press, Inc.

Internationalization of Companies from Developing Countries

INTERNATIONAL BUSINESS PRESS
Erdener Kaynak, PhD
Executive Editor

Internationalization of Companies from Developing Countries

John Kuada
Olav Jull Sørensen

International Business Press®
An Imprint of The Haworth Press, Inc.
New York • London • Oxford

Published by

International Business Press®, an imprint of The Haworth Press, Inc., 10 Alice Street, Binghamton, NY 13904-1580

Cover design by Jennifer M. Gaska.

Library of Congress Cataloging-in-Publication Data

Kuada, John.
    Internationalization of companies from developing countries / John Kuada, Olav Jull Sørensen.
       p. cm.
    Includes bibliographical references.
    ISBN 0-7890-0721-5 (hb : alk. paper) — ISBN 0-7890-1079-8 (pbk.: alk. paper)
    1. International business enterprises—Developing countries. 2. Industrial policy—Developing countries. I. Sørensen, Olav Jull. II. Title.

HD2755.5 .K83 2000
338.8′881724—dc21

                                             99-056494

CONTENTS

Acknowledgments

This book could not have been written without the help and generosity of several people. Our sincere thanks go to all of them. The Ghanaian managers who freely gave of their time to discuss their activities, goals, problems, and achievements with us (sometimes outside their normal working hours and on weekends) deserve our special thanks. We are also grateful to Mrs. Adelaide Kastner and Mr. Daniel O. Tetteh, currently lecturers at the School of Administration, University of Ghana, who served as our research assistants during the data collection phase of the project while they were writing their master's degree theses. We are also indebted to Professor Steven A. Nkrumah, Director of the School of Administration, University of Ghana, for his support and encouragement throughout the project and for warmly accepting our request for research collaboration with the staff of the school. Funding for the data collection in Ghana came from Danish International Development Assistance (DANIDA). We are very grateful for the support.

We sincerely thank our colleagues at the Centre for International Studies, Aalborg University, Aalborg, Denmark, who graciously discussed several drafts of the manuscript with us and compelled us to think through some of our theoretical arguments. In addition, we extend our gratitude to Professor Erdener Kaynak for the profound interest he has shown in the publication of this book and for providing insightful comments on the final draft of the manuscript.

Many other people have helped us prepare the manuscript. We extend our sincere thanks to all of them. In particular, we would like to thank Mrs. Gitte Thomsen for editing the final manuscript and Mrs. Joan Vuust Milborg for preparing the layout.

Finally, we would like to acknowledge our profound gratitude to our families. Without their encouragement and support, the book would not have been completed.

John Kuada
Olav Jull Sørensen
Aalborg, Denmark

ABOUT THE AUTHORS

John Kuada, PhD, is Associate Professor of International Management at the Center for International Studies at Aalborg University in Aalborg, Denmark. Previously, he taught marketing and management subjects at the University of Ghana, the Copenhagen School of Business, and Roskilde University in Denmark. Dr. Kuada has been a visiting scholar at numerous universities in Europe and Africa and has served as a consultant to government organizations and private companies on business-related issues. Currently, his research interests are in intercultural management, cross-national interfirm relations, and international marketing.

Olav Jull Sørensen is Professor of International Business Economics at the Center for International Studies at Aalborg University in Aalborg, Denmark. He is also the Main Coordinator of the masters of science program at the University. A former senior lecturer at the University of Ghana, Mr. Sørensen is the coordinator of a research program to study the integration of Ghanaian companies in the world economy. In addition, he is the president of the International Society on Marketing and Development and chairman of the Scientific Council of INTAS, an EU research program for the former Soviet countries.

Abbreviations

APDF	Africa Project Development Facility
ASEAN	Association of Southeast Asian Nations
CEPS	Customs, Excise, and Preventive Services
DANIDA	Danish International Development Assistance
ECOWAS	Economic Community of West African States
EFC	Export Finance Company
EPZ	export-processing zone
FAGE	Federation of Association of Ghanaian Exporters
FDI	foreign direct investment
FOB	free on board
FTZ	free-trade zone
GBR	government-business relations
GCC	Ghana Chamber of Commerce
GDP	gross domestic product
GEPC	Ghana Export Promotion Council
GIPC	Ghana Investment Promotion Centre

GNCC	Ghana National Chamber of Commerce
GSB	Ghana Standards Board
IESC	International Executive Service Corps
IFC	international finance corporation
IMF	International Monetary Fund
ISSER	Institute of Statistical, Social, and Economic Research (Ghana)
ITC	International Trade Center
JV	joint venture
MIS	management information systems
MNC	multinational corporation
MNE	multinational enterprise
MOTI	Ministry of Trade and Industry
MTP-NTE	Medium-Term Plan for Nontraditional Exports
NAFTA	North American Free Trade Agreement
NIC	newly industrialized country
OECD	Organization for Economic Cooperation and Development
OLI	ownership, location, and internalization
PEED	Private Enterprise and Export Development
PEF	Private Enterprise Foundation
R&D	research and development

SA	strategic alliance
SAP	structural adjustment program
SEZ	special economic zone
SMEs	small- and medium-sized enterprises
SOE	state-owned enterprise
TIP	Trade and Investment Program
TPU	Trade Promotion Unit
USAID	United States Agency for International Development

Introduction

BACKGROUND

Integration of the world economy has long been an issue of significant academic interest. Recent available evidence indicates that significant shifts in trade flows between and among the economic regions of the world must be expected in the coming decades. Although international business will still be centered on the interlinked economies of the Triad—Western Europe, Japan, and North America—the contribution of other countries to world trade, particularly the "tiger" economies of Asia, will grow in significance (Ellis and Williams, 1995). Such distinctive shifts in world business are caused by a combination of external drivers and country-specific policy measures that favor economic liberalization and foreign direct investment. Even in the developing economies of Africa, Latin America, and the rest of Asia, recent economic development policies have been aimed at reducing direct state involvement in business. Restrictive legal and regulatory frameworks are being dismantled, and a gamut of macro- and micro-economic measures are being adopted to encourage private-sector development by both local and foreign investors. China's open-door policies, which began in the early 1980s, are a classic case in point, but similar evidence can be found elsewhere.

Just as the developing countries are opening up their economies to foreign investors, the increased intensity of international competition has pressured firms in the developed market economies to pursue outsourcing strategies and/or direct foreign investments in countries with low labor costs (Dunning, 1989). Others have seen no alternative but to locate in the developing countries or in the transitional economies of Eastern and Central Europe. As Dunning (1989) observes, these firms have become more footloose in their choice of location as their dependence on natural and immobile factor endowments has been reduced. There has also been a marked increase in the adoption of a hybrid of cost-saving collaborative arrangements between firms in developed and developing countries (Borys and Jemison, 1989).

These new developments call for a reappraisal of contemporary internationalization theories to determine the quality of policy and strategy guidelines designed to assist governments and firms in developing countries in their efforts to integrate into the world economy. An understanding of the diverse factors that combine to shape the internationalization process of firms (in both developed and developing countries) is imperative if interfirm collaborative arrangements are to succeed on a sustainable basis.

Research into the internationalization processes of firms based in developing countries is, however, in an embryonic stage. Previous studies have been concentrated on developed country firms. Few studies have been published on constraints to export sector development and performance of exporting firms in developing countries. Two broad categories of constraints have been identified in these studies: (1) preshipment constraints and (2) postshipment constraints. Preshipment constraints cover issues such as input supply, product design, product quality, packaging, as well as shipping and delivery (Lall, 1991). The problems of timely delivery of contracted quantity and quality of inputs have received some attention (Vernon-Wortzel, Wortzel, and Deng, 1988). Additional problems frequently cited are those of poor quality supervision and enforcement in the production process as well as the inability of firms to adapt to the rapid pace of design changes and to make necessary investments that would enable them to fulfill specific preshipment requirements (Lall, 1991). For example, Harris-Pascal, Humphrey, and Dolan (1998) report, from their study of the supply chain management of U.K. horticultural markets, that the major supermarkets and importers in the United Kingdom require their suppliers to possess a broad range of postharvest competencies, such as the management of cooling and cold-storage systems, on-site packaging, and capabilities to ensure high-quality and reliable deliveries, if they are to have any chance of being listed as regular suppliers. Similar observations have been made by Olsen, Biswas, and Kacker (1992), who analyzed the constraints faced by developing country exporters in entering the European Union markets. Although developed country firms face similar preshipment problems, the gravity of such problems is more pronounced in the case of developing country-based firms due to the latter's limited problem-solving resources and capabilities and the limited support offered by their operational environments.

Postshipment constraints are equally serious. Where the exporting firm is unable to sell through an established distributor with substantial coverage of the selected markets, it has to assume responsibility for the distribution and marketing functions of wholesaling, retailing, and after-sales services (in the case of some manufactured products). There are also additional transactional costs of monitoring the marketing process to reduce the incidence of unpleasant surprises from opportunistic overseas channel members.

These considerations underscore the argument that developing country exporters require substantial foreign marketing knowledge to operate successfully in distant markets.[1] However, the contemporary literature on international market knowledge holds that firms acquire their knowledge experientially, i.e., through actions and involvement in the market and not outside it (Johanson and Vahlne, 1977). The inability of developing country firms to acquire sufficient market knowledge is therefore seen as yet another serious constraint on their performance. Thus some writers have argued that these firms should strive to develop solid links with established overseas distributors who can provide them with the required market knowledge. Such links, however, hold the danger of making new developing country exporters very dependent on a single overseas distributor and, accordingly, vulnerable to opportunism.

Although the available studies provide some valuable insights into the problems faced by developing country exporters, researchers have so far ignored the examination of other equally important issues, such as the motives of internationalization, market selection decisions, and responses to public assistance schemes. Furthermore, theoretical viewpoints that have informed studies of internationalization of firms in the developed market economies have not been effectively integrated into the developing country-based studies. This omission seriously limits our understanding of the extent to which the internationalization processes of developing country firms differ from those of the developed countries and restricts the relevance of policy and strategy guidelines in the internationalization literature for firms in the developing countries. Policymakers in developing countries frequently argue that the export potential in their countries is far greater than their export figures show; many firms in these countries are presumed simply to fail to take advantage of the existing export opportunities.

It is against the backdrop of these observations that the value of the present study must be assessed. The study is predicated on the view that a sober and comprehensive analysis of the export behavior of firms in the developing countries is essential for a purposeful, directed strategy aimed at further improvements in the export sector. Thus, our overall objective in this book is to advance the general understanding of the modes of operation of exporting firms in developing countries, drawing specific attention to their perceived problems, strategies, and choices, or lack thereof. This is done by providing theoretical foundations on which investigations of export behaviors of developing country firms can be conducted. The relevance of the theories is discussed and illustrated by empirical information about the process of internationalization of Ghanaian companies. Ghana is chosen as an illustrative country case study to represent the category of developing countries to which the theoretical discussions apply.

STRUCTURE OF THE STUDY

The study is presented in three main parts. As indicated earlier, the theoretical inspirations guiding the study are derived from a review of the contemporary literature in international business. This is the task taken up in Part I. Part II discusses the results of the empirical investigations in detail and presents a conceptual approach to understanding the process of internationalization of Ghanaian firms. Finally, a synthesis of the theories and reflections on the empirical evidence is provided in Part III in the format of a theoretical framework for the internationalization of companies from developing countries.

Chapter 1 outlines the leading theories and models of internationalization.

Chapter 2 discusses the processes by which firms acquire information about foreign markets and build up their international market knowledge. It takes the reader through the contemporary theories of market knowledge generation and discusses them from the viewpoints of three prototype orientations to decision making in management: the "Planning Orientation," the "Action Orientation," and the "Network Orientation."

Chapter 3 discusses the motives underlying firms' decisions to engage in export activities, drawing attention to internal as well as external triggers. The distinction between proactive and reactive motives is also discussed, raising questions as to whether the motives triggering initial decisions continue for long in the internationalization process of the firms. The chapter also discusses the market choice decisions of firms. The reader's attention is drawn to the distinction between the expansive and contractible approaches to market selection as discussed in contemporary literature. It is argued that developing country firms select foreign markets mainly on the basis of information obtained through their social and business networks.

Chapter 4 continues the discussion of key issues in international marketing by drawing attention to the various alternative modes of entering and developing a foreign market. Factors influencing the choice of entry mode are also discussed.

Chapter 5 discusses the concepts of relationship and interaction as they pertain to international business. The importance of relationships between government institutions, which constitute part of the context within which firms operate, and the firms themselves are highlighted. Furthermore, the reader's attention will be drawn to the role of cross-border interfirm relationships in strengthening the competitive positions of firms.

Chapter 6 concludes the theoretical part of the study by exploring the relevance of the theories, models, and issues presented in Chapters 2 through 5 to the internationalization process of firms in developing countries. The main message contained in this chapter is that, with some modifications, the available theories and models can guide research investigations into the export behavior of these firms.

The analysis and discussions of the empirical data are initiated in Chapter 7 by presenting a profile of Ghana, highlighting the political and economic context of the exporting firms as well as recent government export sector development policies. The chapter also provides an overview of the design of the empirical investigation.

Chapter 8 presents a profile of the firms included in the study. This chapter takes the reader through the background and operational history of the firms, their sizes and product lines, their ownership structure and management, as well as the demographic profiles of their owners and managers. This profile serves as a backdrop against which the other aspects of the empirical results are discussed.

The discussion of the motives underlying initial export decisions is taken up in Chapter 9. The question addressed here is whether the export motives conform to the anticipations contained in the theoretical discussion in Chapter 3. The evidence from these data is mixed, and reasons are given in the chapter for the peculiar factors influencing export motives of Ghanaian firms.

Chapter 10 undertakes a combined discussion of three issues: market knowledge generation, market choice decisions, and modes of foreign market entry. This chapter therefore relates the theoretical discussions in Chapters 2 and 4 to the Ghanaian situation. Major differences between theoretical expectations and the empirical evidence on the three issues are extensively discussed.

Chapter 11 returns to the discussion of the local context within which business firms are embedded, an issue previously initiated in Chapter 6. The key issues highlighted in this chapter are the perceptions and interactions between business firms and public institutions and how these affect the tempo of development and overall performance of the firms.

Part III pulls together both the theoretical and empirical discussions in an attempt to offer a conceptual framework for analyzing and understanding the internationalization process of Ghanaian firms and, by extension, firms in developing countries. Chapter 12 stresses the importance of local as well as cross-border interfirm relationships. It introduces the concepts *upstream* and *downstream* internationalization to highlight the different forms of internationalization in which Ghanaian firms may engage, either sequentially or concurrently, to develop their presently weak technological capacity and improve their competitive position. The importance of a supportive local institutional context for effective operation of these firms is also highlighted.

Chapter 13 provides a summary of the main issues discussed in the book and draws attention to their strategy and policy implications.

PART I:
INTERNATIONALIZATION THEORIES AND ISSUES OF DEVELOPING COUNTRY FIRMS

Over the past three decades, a plethora of both conceptual and empirical studies has been published on the export behavior of firms. It is generally accepted that export marketing is by far the most typical type of international business involvement among firms in developed and developing countries. As Cavusgil (1984a) explains, this form of internationalization is less risky and requires less resource commitment than foreign direct investment. Thomas and Araujo's (1985) review of the export behavior research provides an overview of the dominant academic understanding of the field a decade ago. The main points of agreement at that time were the following:

1. Export behavior and foreign market entry decisions can be viewed as innovation adoption behavior; the innovation can be traced to an innovator, i.e., the decision maker in the firm.
2. The export development process proceeds in a sequential, stagelike manner with the tempo of internationalization and the degree of resource commitment, contingent on a number of factors, including individual characteristics of managers.
3. Exporter profiles can be used in ascertaining identifiable characteristics of firms at different stages in the internationalization process.
4. A leading determinant of export behavior is firm size and its related amount of resources and managerial skills.

The authors, however, observed that most of the published studies lacked a generalizable empirical base, since they were cross-sectional and limited in geographical scope and sample size. Furthermore, nearly all the studies implicitly assumed that export is a first step in the internationalization process of firms. Exporting was considered a good thing in its own right, and companies with the enabling conditions and opportunities would enter export business. As the subsequent discussions will show, some of these viewpoints have been subjected to vigorous criticism in the more recent literature. Strandskov's (1995) literature review indicates that a number of new competing theoretical perspectives have emerged, creating a pluralistic base for studies in export behavior. Thus, studies in international business today cannot derive their theoretical inspiration from a single accepted framework. Leonidou and Katsikeas (1996) drew similar conclusions in their review of three decades of export marketing research.

The differences in theoretical viewpoints expressed in the literature, however, provide the researcher with the advantage of searching widely for an appropriate angle of analysis, although at the risk of reducing the general acceptability of empirical results based on each of the viewpoints.

The present study is mindful of these theoretical opportunities and weaknesses. As intimated earlier, this part of the book aims to

1. place the study within the existing frame of knowledge in the area and
2. examine the degree of consistency of the empirical results presented here with the major theoretical viewpoints in the existing literature.

This is done, first, by undertaking a review of the mainstream theories of internationalization and, second, by discussing their applicability to the analysis of the export activities of developing country firms.

Chapter 1

Theories and Models
of Internationalization

This chapter provides an overview of the contemporary theories of internationalization of firms and discusses their underlying meta-theoretical assumptions. The theories have been grouped into three categories, each emphasizing a specific view of the firm's perception of its "environment" and means of dealing with it.

CATEGORIZATION OF THEORIES
OF INTERNATIONALIZATION

Companies seeking to internationalize should consider two questions: Why do they want to internationalize? How will they achieve internationalization? Theories dealing with the internationalization of companies are many, and the two questions—why and how—are answered using diverse scientific approaches. In this study, the theory models are grouped into the following three categories:

- Stages Models (the universal path of internationalization)
- Contingency Models (the adaption-planning approach to internationalization)
- (Inter)Action Models (internationalization achieved by seizing international opportunities through networking)

These three categories reflect important differences in the understanding of a company's internationalization process. These differences can be illustrated by looking at the categories in terms of the following:

1. An objective versus a subjective worldview
2. A static versus a dynamic perspective
3. A planning versus an action orientation

Objective versus Subjective Worldview

An objective worldview implies that the theory (i.e., the researcher) assumes that the business world, including the international markets, exists independently of the individual businessperson. It also implies that the theory assumes that the business world behaves according to general (natural) laws and principles that can be determined through scientific investigations, thereby increasing one's knowledge of internationalization.

A subjective worldview implies that the theory assumes that the business world is a social construction, i.e., created by the actions and interaction of human beings. No general laws of behavior can be found because each and every situation is unique. Thus, knowledge, in the natural science sense of the term, cannot be accumulated. Of importance are the perceptions and actions of individual businesspeople.

Static versus Dynamic Perspective

A static approach implies that the theory provides a snapshot of the situation. This contrasts with a dynamic approach, which, in a simple version, implies the addition of a time dimension. This means the internationalization activities are described at different points in time. This version of the dynamic approach is called the "comparative static approach."

A dynamic approach may also imply that it is not time, as such, that is of interest but rather the dynamic processes, e.g., the interaction between an exporter and an importer that gradually enhances the company's internationalization.

Planning versus Action Orientation

The theories of internationalization may also be grouped according to whether they focus attention mainly on management planning activities or are more concerned with managers' actions and experiences. For example, theories related to the selection of markets or market entry modes may be considered planning tools. Here, the starting point is the totality of markets or market entry modes, the totality being gradually reduced using a stepwise selection procedure. As will be noted subsequently (see Chapter 3), market analysis presupposes that the company needs information for the planning of its activities.

In contrast, action-oriented theories have the intuitive idea of the businessperson as the starting point. The idea is followed up by immediate actions, which in turn provide the actors with experience. This experience is then turned into knowledge through a process of reflections (Kuada and Sørensen, 1997). (Table 1.1 provides an overview of the metascientific bases of the three categories of theories.)

The Stages and Contingency Models belong to mainstream thinking within business economics, assuming an objective reality that science can reveal and present as an input to the corporate planning activities. The models are static or comparatively static, focusing on the situation at a specific point in time and/or extending the past into the future.

TABLE 1.1. Metascientific Dimensions of the Theories of Internationalization

Scientific Dimension	Stages Models	Contingency Models	(Inter)Action Models
Objective versus subjective world-view	Objective	Objective	Subjective (shared understanding)
Static versus dynamic perspective	Comparison of static analysis at each stage	Static	Dynamic
Planning versus action orientation	Planning	Planning	Interaction
Managerial implications	Identify present stage; prepare and plan for the next	Build and use analytical capability	Build and use social capital, i.e., interaction capability

In contrast, the (Inter)Action Models view internationalization as a social construction process. Universal laws on which companies can base their planning do not exist, but through interaction, the companies may adopt a common worldview, i.e., an intersubjective, agreed-upon mode of behavior. Planning is not ruled out of this perspective, but actions/interactions and the concomitant accumulation of experience are more important than the speculations associated with planning. In other words, internationalization is not planned; it is acted/enacted/interacted.

Each of the three categories of internationalization theories are discussed in the subsequent sections, and examples of theories falling within each category are presented.

THE STAGES MODELS

The Stages Models view the internationalization of a company as a sequential and orderly process. The company moves through a set of stages, with each stage providing the necessary international prerequisites for the company to move to the next stage. The Stages Models provide us with a generalized pattern that may be used to predict and plan a company's internationalization. According to the model, managers decide on their international activities by first identifying the stage in which the company is currently positioned and then preparing the company to move into the next predetermined stage.

The existing Stages Models can be divided into two types:

1. Models showing internationalization to be based on learning and the accumulation of experience—the Learning Stages Theory
2. Models showing internationalization to be based on adaption to changes in the environment, i.e., to changes in supply, demand, and competition—the International Product Life Cycle Theory

The Learning Stages Theory

Although heavily criticized (Turnbull, 1987), the Learning Stages Theory of the internationalization process is still a dominant model in contemporary international business literature.[1] Many versions of this theory can be found, but the underlying philosophy is the same for all versions: the internationalization of a company is an orderly and sequential process in which the shift from one stage to the next is based on the learning and accumulation of experience within the preceding stage.

The many versions of the theory differ as to the number of stages a company moves through in the transition from a domestically oriented company to a full-fledged global company. The versions also differ in relation to their focus: some emphasize a specific factor, such as the market entry and development mode (Johanson and Wiedersheim-Paul, 1975); some focus attention on market selection (Bilkey and Tesar, 1977); yet others focus on the general engagement in, and commitment to, internationalization. Three versions of the Learning Stages Theory are shown in Table 1.2.

TABLE 1.2. Three Versions of the Learning Stages Theory of Internationalization

Stage	Market Entry and Development Mode (Johanson and Widersheim-Paul, 1975)	Market Choice (Bilkey and Tesar, 1977)	Export Involvement and Resource Commitment (Cavusgil, 1984a)
1	No exports	No exports	No exports
2	Export via agent	Filling unsolicited export orders	Experimental involvement, e.g., passive response, applying domestic marketing strategies abroad, little financial commitment, etc.
3	Export via sales subsidiary	Exploring the feasibility of exporting	Active involvement, e.g., active search, adaptation to foreign markets, commitment of resources, etc.
4	Production in a subsidiary abroad	Exports on an experimental basis to psychologically close countries	Committed involvement, e.g., global search for exports, long-term commitments, and foreign direct investment (FDI).
5		Experienced exporter who adjusts to market and country diversity	
6		Exports to psychologically distant countries	

Critics point out that the Learning Stages Theory basically focuses on the pattern of internationalization, thereby ignoring the context in which the internationalization takes place. In other words, the internationalization of a company is assumed to be context-free: the same pattern is expected across different contexts and environments. Furthermore, the different versions tend not to deal with the actual foundation on which the theory is based, i.e., the learning aspect and the accumulation of knowledge. The different authors (with the exception of Johanson and Vahlne, 1977) are preoccupied with the outcome of learning, i.e., the actual development of the international engagement in terms of number and types of markets, entry modes, organization modes, methods of market research, etc. (Sørensen, 1991; Kuada and Sørensen, 1995).

An important question to ask is, "Why is it that a general pattern of internationalization can be found?" The question is relevant, considering that each and every company is making an attempt to be different from its competitors, i.e., to develop a unique competitive advantage. If all companies strive to be unique, it appears quite unlikely that a common pattern or a universal law can be found to describe the internationalization of firms.

Three tentative explanations may be offered for the appearance of a general pattern of internationalization:

1. According to the rationale of the Stages Models, internationalization is based on the laws and principles of learning combined with risk taking. A company learns from its actions, and when it has acquired enough experience and reached an acceptable risk level, it is ready to take another step on the internationalization path. As all companies follow this rule of risk reduction through learning, a common internationalization pattern emerges.
2. Related to the first explanation, a general pattern may also be found either because companies are managed by people who have acquired the same management philosophy and the same management tools or because companies learn from one another and imitate the behavior of more successful companies at any given point in time. In these instances, a common pattern will emerge based on common worldviews and, in general, the emergence of a common business culture or system (Whitley, 1992).

The remarkable performance of many Japanese companies on the global market without the use of Western approaches to management is a clear indication that no universal approach to management exists.

3. A general pattern may also be explained by the structure of an industry. For example, a general pattern of development will emerge in industry structures that include many small autonomous companies that are influenced by common social relations. An example is the well-known product life cycle, which reflects the numerous consumers who autonomously, but under social influence, decide to adopt a certain product. In this case, a combination of structural forces and social influence leads to a common pattern of behavior.

Thus, the combination of the presence of many actors and a social interaction without social control lays the foundation for the emergence of general patterns of internationalization. The laws, however, are not natural laws; they are laws based on the mechanisms of social relations.

Transferring this line of thinking to the internationalization of companies, we expect to find general patterns of internationalization in industries with numerous small-scale companies. If such an industry becomes more concentrated, each company possesses the resources to outline its own mode of internationalization and the common pattern is substituted for each company's unique road to the international markets.

The International Product Life Cycle Theory

In 1966, Vernon presented his explanation of why nations trade by way of a theory modeled on the basis of the product life cycle concept. For its time, it was an advanced theory because it simultaneously provided a rationale for trade and foreign investments as orderly, sequential processes. (Theories of foreign direct investment were in their infancy when Vernon presented his Stages Models.)

According to the International Product Life Cycle Theory, a company's internationalization can be divided into three stages: (1) new product, (2) maturing product, and (3) standardized product.

New Product Stage

The theory is concerned with high-income or labor-saving products made initially in advanced market economies, e.g., in the United States. The new products are developed and marketed primarily in the domestic market, but soon these products are exported on a small scale to other advanced market economies, e.g., in Europe.

Maturing Product Stage

The growing markets, the increase in competition, and the standardization of the products give rise to relocation of the production from the home country to larger foreign markets. Other countries may now be served from the home base or from the new production base abroad, depending on the production and transaction costs.

Standardized Product Stage

This is the term used by Vernon (1966) for the mature-decline stage. Production may now be relocated to developing countries, with products being shipped back to the home country as well as to other markets.

Whereas the Learning Stages Theory focuses on the endogenous learning process, the International Product Life Cycle Theory is based on pure economic rationales, i.e., exports versus investments and costs (through location) versus revenues (through market shifts).

In its original form, the life cycle theory may be less useful today. In many instances, production and marketing are global from the very beginning. Multinational corporations (MNCs) use their global production networks, and the products are marketed at least in the core countries of the Triad market region of North America, Western Europe, and Japan.

Originally, both types of Stages Models were empirically based, and they quickly became popular due to their simplicity and universality. However, over the years they have lost steam. It became clear that no universal path from a domestic to a global company could be found. Some critiques of the theories are as follows:

- Often companies do not have a consolidation period at home before going international.
- At times, companies skip certain stages.
- At times, companies decide to reverse, i.e., moving from a higher to a lower commitment stage.
- Often companies do not move beyond a certain stage.

Although criticized, the Learning Stages Theory is still popular because it is based on learning and the accumulation of experience and not just on economic rationales. Although no longer considered a universal theory, it may still prove useful as a reference model against which a company's international position and future moves can be discussed, although not determined and decided upon.

THE CONTINGENCY MODELS

The Nature of Contingency Models

Contingency Models of companies' internationalization have partly been formulated as a critique of the dominant Stages Models (Turnbull, 1987). The Contingency Models state that the internationalization of a company is dependent on the environment, especially in regard to demand conditions, industry structure, and government policies. No generalized pattern for the internationalization of companies can therefore be expected; the internationalization process is distinct for each and every industry, and perhaps even for individual companies.

Contingency Models, which date back to the 1950s, made a major breakthrough in management with Lawrence and Lorsch's (1967) work on organizational adaptation to environmental circumstances. A substantial part of contemporary marketing literature endorses this line of thought, concerning itself with how the environment shapes marketing programs and organization. Thus, Contingency Models of internationalization form part of the general discussion on how environmental structure and conditions determine company strategy, or vice versa.

Contingency Models include three basic components: (1) a set of *environmental factors,* i.e., a model of the environment in which the company operates, which defines (2) the *opportunities*, i.e., the alternatives available to the company, which, in turn, are affected by (3) the *decision criteria* of the company, reflecting the management preferences and allocation of company resources.

The relevant set of decision criteria is well known. The most important criteria are maximize profit, minimize costs, achieve maximum control over international activities, maintain maximum market share, and minimize financial risks. Other more secondary criteria may be effectiveness, flexibility, and information feedback.

From a management point of view, Contingency Models imply that the firm is viewed as an open system and that there is no one best way of internationalizing the company. The task of management is to achieve the best fit between a more or less turbulent, and perhaps hostile, environment, with its threats and opportunities, and the company's internal resources (strengths and weaknesses). This involves analyzing the situation, defining the decision criteria (costs, information, etc.), working out alternatives, and using the decision criteria to select the optimal alternative. Thus, a company's analytical capacity is crucial to the planning of its internationalization. In general, Contingency Models are in line with (if not identical to) the planning approach, i.e., the rational mode of thinking.

Contingency Models are numerous but can be divided into two basic groups:

1. Conditional Models that specify relationships between dependent and independent variables and
2. Conceptual Framework Models

Conditional Models first stipulate the independent variables or conditions, followed by the action to be taken if the conditions are fulfilled. A notable example is the Eclectic Paradigm suggested by Dunning (1988) that stipulates the conditions to be fulfilled for a company to make a foreign direct investment.

Conceptual Framework Models, on the other hand, describe the environment by a set of concepts or factors to be taken into consideration in making a strategic decision. They do not, however, stipulate the action to be taken by the company. One may say that they stipulate an action space, defined by the conceptual framework. An example of such a model is Porter's (1990) "diamond model" of the competitive advantage of nations that requests the researcher to analyze the environment or part of it, e.g., an industry, in terms of factor and demand conditions, supporting industries, the structure of the industry, and the strategies pursued by the firms. Such an analysis is expected to provide an understanding of the situation, including the general space for actions. Thus, Conceptual Framework Models connote ways of thinking about the general situation and, perhaps, the procedure for carrying out an analysis of the situation, but they do not provide well-defined answers or strategic actions due to the complexity of the environment.

Externalization and Internalization Across Borders

The dominant Contingency Models related to the internationalization of companies have their roots in Coase's ideas of the boundary of the firm (Coase, 1937). Coase aimed to answer the question, What constitutes a company? This is not the key question here, but when companies internationalize, the boundary of a company is constantly being moved, either by internalization or externalization of activities. In fact, externalization or internalization of activities across borders is presently one of the dominant modes of gaining competitive advantage. For example, companies can generate competitive advantage by subcontracting some of their products or components to companies located in countries with low labor costs. This approach is commonly referred to in international business literature as outsourcing, or an externalization of activities. Alternatively, companies internalize activities by investing in marketing or production facilities abroad.

Contingency Models are concerned not just with exports but also with foreign investment and imports (sourcing). In general, the models reflect the debate on internalization versus externalization of activities, i.e., whether to carry out an activity in house or buy from/ sell through the market. The essence of this debate is best explained through a discussion of internalization and externalization theories.

Internalization Theories

Internalization through foreign direct investments (FDIs) is a key concept in both Dunning's Eclectic Paradigm (Dunning, 1988) and Williamson's Transaction Costs Theory (Williamson, 1979, 1981;

Douma and Schreuder, 1991). Both views aim to address under what conditions a company will internalize an activity. Williamson's formula is based on two human factors, bounded rationality and opportunism, and two environmental factors, uncertainty and industry structure. Given specific configurations of the four factors, a company will opt for the internalization solution; i.e., the activity will be part of the hierarchical governance structure.[2] Dunning's Eclectic Paradigm provides an answer by way of the OLI formula, which states that a company will invest abroad if it possesses ownership (O), location (L), and internalization (I) advantages.

It should be noted that the Transaction Costs Theory does not explicitly deal with the internalization of companies. However, its rationale, based on the four factors, is equally valid across borders as it is within the boundary of any single market economy.

Externalization Theories

With some justification, the previous two theories may be said to deal with both internalization and externalization. If, according to the theories, it does not pay to internalize, per definition, the firms externalize the activity; i.e., the activity is performed by other companies with whom the company in question establishes market relations. However, as shown next, due to their assumptions, the theories cannot address all aspects of the externalization issue.

Turning to the concept of externalization, it can be noted that the tendency to outsource has been as strong as the tendency to engage in FDIs. Outsourcing is related to both upstream and downstream activities and, in recent years, has gathered extra momentum due to the general globalization of the economy. However, current opinion suggests that the advantages of outsourcing are fewer than expected (Sørensen, 1996b).

Basically, companies outsource internationally for two reasons:

1. To capture static efficiency, especially by exploiting low labor costs. In this case, the company must stay flexible because the world map of low-labor-cost enclaves changes constantly. Related to static efficiency is the issue of economies of scale that independent market actors can exploit.

2. To benefit from dynamic efficiency, i.e., to exploit the innovativeness of other companies and, for example, industrial districts. Today, many products are based on a portfolio of technologies, and a company cannot be in the lead in all cases. To stay competitive, a company outsources innovation by, for example, entering into strategic alliances with innovative subsuppliers.

The most well-known theory on externalization is the Theory of Lean Production, which is related especially to the upstream activities of a company (Lamming, 1993). By outsourcing few or many of the activities of the value chain, a company becomes leaner, functioning, in effect, similar to a trading firm, while reducing costs and stimulating innovation. The principal way to do this is to organize one or more tiers of subsuppliers, some of which are simple suppliers of standard components, while others are the innovative wing of the company in question.

Compared to the Stages Models, the Contingency Models broaden the concept of internationalization. Whereas the Stages Models are concerned only with downstream activities, the Contingency Models are also dealing with internationalization through upstream activities, i.e., through global sourcing and outsourcing.

Another difference is that the Stages Models are based on learning theory whereas the OLI formula and the Transaction Costs Theory are based on economic rationales. The Transaction Costs Theory sets out to choose the governance structure (market or hierarchy) operating at the lowest costs. The Theory of Lean Production is also based on an economic rationale, but the economic activities are to some extent embedded in long-term social relations and innovative activities that are extremely difficult to manage using pure economic formulas.

THE (INTER)ACTION MODELS

Core Concepts of (Inter)Action Models

Broadly speaking, (Inter)Action Models belong to the field of economic sociology, according to which economic activity has a social dimension (Granovetter and Swedberg, 1992). The models generally criticize conventional economics literature as "dehuman-ized." That is, it ignores human beings or assumes that economic activities are carried out by actors with no memory of their previous actions. They argue instead that economic activities are embedded in social relations: "An action by a member of a network is embedded, because it is expressed in interaction with other people" (Ibid., p. 9).

To illustrate, in economics, price formation is purely a question of the forces of demand and supply. By accepting that social relations matter, the actual social connection between identifiable buyers and sellers influences the formation of the price.

Whereas Contingency Models assume that, at company level, each and every situation may be unique and planning, by necessity, must be based on a detailed analysis of the situation, the (Inter)Action Models are action based; they view the market as composed of a set of identifiable and autonomous actors who continuously interact and, through their interaction, build long-term social relations. When such regular or daily contacts and long-term relations exist, the set of actors is said to constitute a network.

In essence, this means that a specific company's relations to other companies can be classified as short term, i.e., arm's-length market relations, and long term, i.e., network relations. The (Inter)Action Models deal only with the long-term relations, which are believed to be the most crucial for the company.

The critical question is, Why do companies build long-term relationships? A quick answer could be because companies involve human beings, who, by nature, are social beings and are thus more or less defined by the social relations they have, i.e., not by who they are but by whom they know.

The answer provided by network theorists is that through long-term relationships, companies gain access to resources controlled by others. That is, the Network Theory, unlike the Stages Models, does not believe in the formula of building endogenous resources followed by conquering the market. They argue that companies build resources through the interaction with other actors, thereby gaining access to the resources of others.

In the process of building resources, the companies adapt to each other and gradually become interdependent; i.e., each company's resources become linked to the other's to the benefit of both parties.

For example, the production planning system of a company may be adapted to the need for just-in-time deliveries to customers.

Although focus is on the process of building, maintaining, and dissolving long-term relations, a key concept in the (Inter)Action Models is the position of a company within the network. Basically, a company's position defines its present control over, and access to, network resources. However, position also defines a company's future opportunities. One of the distinct features of a network is that while, on the one hand, it handles the daily routines established between actors, this daily interaction, on the other hand, creates and exposes the actors to new opportunities.

Obviously, a company can influence its own position and, thus, the extent to which it is exposed to new opportunities. The position in relation to the information flow in the network is crucial. If a company has relations to actors with access to the same type of information, it may have an extensive network, but its exposure to new opportunities is limited compared to a company that consciously has established relations to actors possessing different information.

This naturally brings us to the question, What do the (Inter)Action Models and the Network Theory of the market have to offer in terms of understanding and explaining the process of internationalization and the international position of a company?

The (Inter)Action Models define internationalization as an extension of a company's present action space to include interaction with companies abroad. Such extensions of the network across borders are the result of an actor's present position in the network and the actual seizing of opportunities arising from the present network interaction. Thus, the internationalization of a company emerges from the continuous, daily interaction among the members of the network. In other words, present network members are used as stepping stones into foreign countries.

The (Inter)Action Models may be viewed as Contingency Models in the sense that the internationalization of a company depends on the position of the company in the network. The internationalization of companies, according to the (Inter)Action Models, is an evolutionary process whereby the network, through the continuous interaction of its members, is gradually changed and restructured to include actors abroad. From a management perspective, the task of the international manager is to position the company in the network so that opportunities to establish relations to new (and resourceful) actors abroad are revealed. Accessibility to information offered by other network members enables a company to identify opportunities quickly and to take advantage of them, granting that they have the required resources to exploit them (Burt, 1992; Sørensen, 1995).

The Network Approach to Internationalization (The Uppsala Version)

Based on network thinking, researchers from Uppsala University in Sweden have developed a model for the internationalization of companies (Johanson and Mattsson, 1988). According to this approach, a company can internationalize in three ways:

1. By extension, i.e., establish relations to actors/networks in new markets
2. By penetration, i.e., deepen and strengthen relations in existing networks abroad
3. By coordination, i.e., improve the relations between actors in different networks in different markets

The internationalization model developed by the Swedish researchers is less process oriented than most writings on networks; rather, it builds on the position of a company in the industry. The company's internationalization depends on its own position in the network, i.e., how international the company is compared to other actors, as well as the general degree of internationalization of the industry and market (see Table 1.3). Combining the two dimensions, a matrix appears, with the following four different network positions.

TABLE 1.3. Internationalization and the Network Approach

		Degree of Market Internationalization	
		Low	High
Degree of Firm Internationalization	Low	The Early Starter	The Late Starter
	High	The Lonely International	The International Among Others

The Early Starter

The early starter has no links to actors abroad and must break new ground because no other companies have established such links. Only indirect links may exist, for example, via the company's suppliers or customers. If such indirect links do not exist and cannot be used as stepping stones into new markets, the company will have to work from scratch, i.e., identify actors and develop relations, for example, by attending exhibitions abroad or by contacting a number of potential links from a list prepared by someone such as the commercial attaché of the country's embassy. The company should expect some difficulties in establishing links because the industry (including the customers) is not internationally oriented.

The Lonely International

The company in question has acquired international experience of its own, but its competitors and customers, i.e., its network partners, are still mainly domestically oriented. By using the networks established as an early starter, as well as the international experience acquired in that process, the company may build new relations in new markets or penetrate deeper into present ones by building more and stronger ties to the present actors in the country. Again, the internationalizing company will face problems in developing relations abroad, as the industry is not very international, but compared to the early starter position, the lonely international company has the advantage of having experience in breaking into foreign domestic networks, thus gaining "first-mover advantages."

The Late Starter

Here, the other companies comprising the industry have already established long-term relations to actors abroad, while the focal company has remained domestically oriented. The problem is not identifying actors with an international orientation but rather finding actors who have not already established long-term relations with actors abroad. To break into such well-structured, international networks, the company may, if it has the necessary financial resources, acquire a partner abroad, or it may have a specialized product that is able to carve a niche in the market.

The International Among Others

With all companies being international, each company can strengthen its position by building stronger ties to present actors or by coordinating the various links in different countries. That is, the company develops competitiveness through reorganizing the value chain, exploiting economies of scale, and standardizing activities.

SUMMARY

This chapter provided an overview of the key concepts, theories, and models of internationalization found in the existing literature. It discussed their metatheoretical foundations as well as differences in their focuses and strategy implications. Three categories of models were presented: (1) Stages Models, (2) Contingency Models, and (3) (Inter)Action Models. The Stages Models endorse the view that firms create resources internally and within their domestic markets before embarking on an internationalization process. They tend to internationalize gradually and sequentially, acquiring international market knowledge incrementally as they proceed. Contingency Models, on the other hand, emphasize internal and external conditions that trigger firms' decisions to internationalize either through exports or foreign direct investments. They stress the understanding that firms are open systems, responding to opportunities and threats in the external environment. The (Inter)Action Models take this perspective even further. They stress that firms are not merely open to external impulses but also are actively engaged in the social processes of their ambient environment. By influencing the environment through their interactions with other actors, they, in effect, enact their environments. The concept "embeddedness" was coined to describe the process of actions and interactions among firms. The discussions also highlighted the Network Theory of understanding the internationalization process, drawing attention to the issue of resource creation and sharing among firms within a network.

These theories and models are based on studies of the internationalization process of developed country-based firms. Their relevance in a developing country context is discussed in detail in Chapter 6.

Chapter 2

International Market
Information Acquisition
and Knowledge Generation

ESTABLISHING THE RELEVANCE
OF KNOWLEDGE GENERATION
AND ACCUMULATION

Information and knowledge are crucial for the enterprise in the process of becoming international, and both are key concepts in economics and the development of theories of international business. Considering that internationalization means acting in a hitherto geographically, politically, economically, and culturally unknown space, information becomes the only source on which to base the company's decisions. Per definition, the company has no prior international experience of its own when acting in the new space, and unless it hires someone with such experience from previous jobs, the company can only rely on information already available or to be actively collected by the company. However, information alone is not enough. The information must be analyzed and interpreted for it to make sense to the decision maker. In the end, the perceptions of the decision maker regarding the information lead to the international actions taken by a company.

When exporters move into unknown space, they start accumulating experience. Decisions now are not based solely on information; the markets can be assessed on the basis of a company's own experience. However, as with information, experience normally cannot stand alone. Only through a process of interpretation and reflection does experience become knowledge on which to base the steps to follow on the internationalization path.

Therefore, access to information and the opportunity to acquire experience and generate knowledge are crucial in a company's internationalization. A useful starting point for discussing the information and knowledge acquisition process of a firm is to examine the behavior of the decision makers. After all, it is the decision maker who determines what and how much information to collect and analyze.

THEORIES OF MARKET KNOWLEDGE GENERATION

Having established the relevance of market information and knowledge generation, the question is, What theoretical models and empirical findings exist that can provide some insight into the issue? First, a taxonomy for the sources of information and knowledge will be outlined. This is then followed by the presentation of three different types of decision makers, each with a different need for and mode of collecting information.

The starting point may be found in the neoclassical theory of the perfect competitive market, in which it is assumed that all market actors have the same and complete information; i.e., no uncertainty and no asymmetrical information exist. Where to mark the finishing line is more difficult. Presently, the strategic planning rationale dominates the thinking within business economics, but a rationale with the firm as "knowledge producer and seller" is emerging, as indicated in an increasing number of studies on "learning organizations" (Pedler, Burgoyne, and Boydell, 1991; Senge, 1990). The learning perspective on companies involves the questions of how companies generate knowledge and how knowledge is transferred or sold, i.e., the market for knowledge.

It is already well established theoretically that the market often fails when a firm wants to sell tacit knowledge. The Transaction Costs Theory has amply demonstrated that tacit knowledge gives rise to internalization. However, Michalet (1991) and Dunning (1995) point out that internalization may not be the optimal governance structure in industries dominated by knowledge-generating firms. An alternative approach is for international firms to form networks or strategic alliances across nations to ensure effective generation and dissemination of information and knowledge. Thus, interfirm coalitions become the dominating governance structure in "the post-globalization economy" and "alliance capitalism." Admittedly, their vision is not based solely on knowledge as the key source of competitive advantage, but knowledge is the major force behind the restructuring of MNCs. The theory of the learning organization, as such, will not be presented and applied here, but the concept of learning does form an essential part of the arguments presented.

Sources of Information for Knowledge Generation

Companies can generate knowledge in four different ways. They can learn from their own direct market actions (source 1). That is, companies can, for example, undertake experiments designed to gain experience that can then be used to enhance further action. (Figure 2.1 provides an overview of sources of information entering the knowledge-generating process in the firms.) Instead of taking direct action, companies may either actively search for and collect data through market research to learn more about the situation or behave passively by being alert to incoming information (source 2). Rather than generating knowledge on their own, companies may acquire it from another source that already possesses the knowledge (source 3). For example, a company could hire a salesperson with the required market-specific knowledge or send managers to attend a seminar on "how to go international." A company may also generate knowledge from within (source 4). For example, a task force may be directed to compile and analyze scattered market knowledge within the company.

Having identified the basic sources of knowledge, the successive steps are to systematize the experience acquired and information collected. This might be done within the framework of formal management information systems (MIS) through the creation of data banks within the company and through developing systems that ensure effective information flow to decision makers at different levels of the company. If knowledge is acquired by an entrepreneurial company, the owner/manager may be the MIS, i.e., the know-how center of the company.

Systematization is, however, not enough. Experience, information, and transferred know-how do not become relevant knowledge until managerial reflections and interpretations have taken place.

FIGURE 2.1. Production of Know-How in a Company Perspective

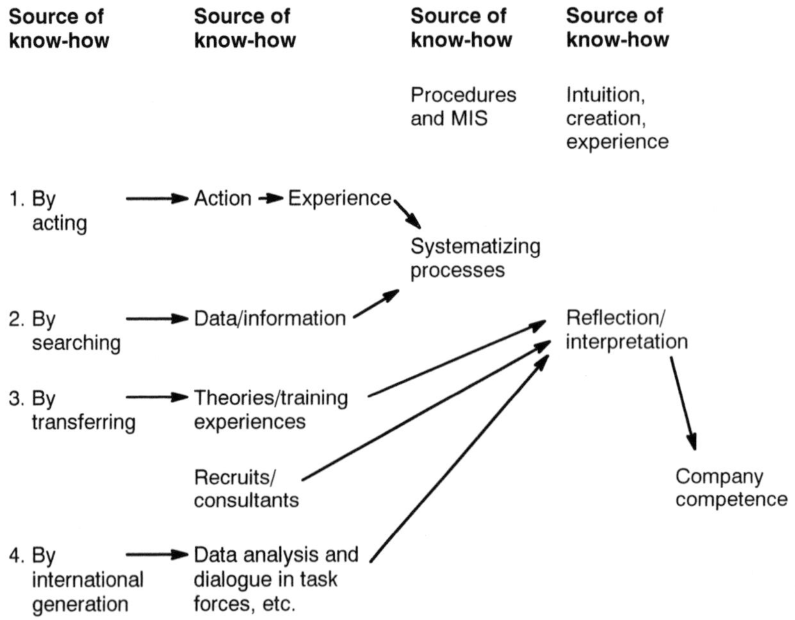

Source of know-how	Source of know-how	Source of know-how	Source of know-how
		Procedures and MIS	Intuition, creation, experience

1. By acting ——▶ Action ➔ Experience

Systematizing processes

2. By searching ——▶ Data/information

Reflection/ interpretation

3. By transferring ——▶ Theories/training experiences

Recruits/ consultants

Company competence

4. By international generation ——▶ Data analysis and dialogue in task forces, etc.

Source: Adapted from Sørensen and Nedergaard, 1993, p. 5.

These processes are guided by present know-how, creativity, and intuition.

Three Prototypes of Decision Makers

To stress the relevance of information and knowledge generation, the focus in the following discussion is not on the sources of information but on the decision makers who use the information obtained from a variety of sources. Decision makers, who decide what and how much information is to be collected, are represented here by three prototypes: the Planning Man, the Action Man, and the Networker.

The Planning Man

Neoclassical economic theories assume that human beings are rational decision makers. That is, they base their choices on careful evaluation of alternatives available to them. The term "Economic Man" is usually used to describe this type of human behavior. In theory, the "Economic Man" is assumed to have access to all information relevant to his decision. In practice, people make decisions under conditions of uncertainty and are therefore constrained in their rationality. The term "Planning Man" is therefore the closest one can get in practice to the neoclassical economic concept of "Economic Man." The Planning Man relies on science-based market research, i.e., the application of rational analytical tools. Information is considered objective; it is collected and analyzed by neutral persons, and its degree of representativeness, validity, and reliability is clearly stated. The research results form part of the corporate planning process. When the market research report reaches the decision maker, the information is filtered; i.e., the decision maker perceives the world, not through his or her own experience, but through the market research reports. Plans formulated on the basis of these reports aim at reducing the uncertainties of the decision maker. In sum, the Planning Man uses the conventional approach to international knowledge generation.

The Action Man

For the Action Man, intuition is quickly followed by action. Little, if any, information is collected before acting. In turn, the action, per definition, gives rise to experience. However, experience is not knowledge. Knowledge derives from experience on which actors have reflected. Unreflected experience takes the form of anecdotes, at best, and has limited relevance in management decision making.

The Action Man copes with international uncertainty and bounded rationality by substituting action preparedness for planning capability. Continuous monitoring and an intuitive feel for potential business, combined with a capacity to act, allow the Action Man to manage his way through, rather than a priori reduce, uncertainty and bounded rationality.

The idea to theoretically pursue the underlying rationale for the Action Man came from studies of the internationalization of small- and medium-sized enterprises (SMEs) in Denmark. The studies revealed that the firms did not use conventional market research before making decisions. They were much more action oriented and relied on personal contacts.

This finding gave rise to two alternative reactions. As a supplier of postgraduate courses, one might conclude that SMEs constitute a prosperous market for courses in how to conduct international market research. Alternatively, as a researcher, one might be puzzled and start searching for the rationale behind the behavior of the SMEs. Should their failure to conduct market research be attributed to their lack of skills or financial resources? Or do they simply consider an alternative approach to market knowledge acquisition as more rewarding? An earlier study (Kuada and Sørensen, 1997) argued that these firms prefer to use "the action approach" to the generation of international knowledge. That is, they act as "the Action Man," progressing through the following steps in knowledge acquisition:

Idea generation → Action → Experience → Reflection/Interpretation → Knowledge

In brief, the model suggests that key decision makers in SMEs initiate their market knowledge generation with ideas that they have about the focal markets. These ideas prompt them to take actions from which they acquire experience. These experiences are then transformed into knowledge after thorough reflection and interpretation. Thus, the rationale for the action approach to knowledge generation includes three elements: a structural component, a human inclination, and a cost consideration:

1. Structurally, it is not possible to keep track of all opportunities and risks in the international market. Bounded rationality limits knowledge generation, but action capacity can compensate for bounded rationality, and acquired experience, if reflected, provides the firm with new knowledge.
2. Action orientation is not a general human inclination, but some people seem to be predisposed to learning through action, other people learn through planning, and still others may like to talk

about plans and actions but do neither of them. Thus, action and planning can mutually substitute for each other; i.e., high action capacity can compensate for low planning capacity, and vice versa.

3. The Action Man economizes on transaction costs by foregoing investigation costs (Buckley, 1990). Or, put another way, the Action Man investigates the market through market activity and generates market knowledge through reflected experience. The extent to which an Action Man approach is less costly than a Planning Man approach depends on managers' ability to combine "selling activity" with "experience reflection." According to Johansson and Nonaka (1987), Japanese managers seem to be able to make better decisions using an Action Man-oriented approach. Rather than relying on and reading formal market research, Japanese managers visit the focal markets and potential customers to get a firsthand impression of them.

Such direct contacts and perceptions constitute valuable sources of knowledge on which to base internationalization strategies, especially when a company is entering markets with unfamiliar cultures.

The Networker

Whereas the Planning Man and the Action Man face more or less hostile environments described in terms of forces rather than actors (i.e., the invisible hand), the Networker is a member of a network of identifiable and visible actors with whom long-term relations have been, or can be, established.

The Networker is well informed about network partners and has rather personal relations with them. The daily interaction and dialogue within the network continuously provides the Networker with pertinent information. When crucial decisions must be made, such as the decision to internationalize, the Networker will consult a few key and trustworthy informants within the network.

The Networker copes with uncertainty and bounded rationality by being well informed through active participation in the network, rather than being an outside strategic observer, and by building long-term relations of trust and mutual orientation that eliminate opportunistic inclinations.

SUMMARY

This chapter highlighted the importance of market knowledge to firms' international business decisions. It also discussed approaches to market knowledge acquisition, with special focus on the decision maker's dispositions. Three decision-maker prototypes were described: the Planning Man, the Action Man, and the Networker. The Planning Man bases decisions on information obtained through survey methods, the Action Man relies on experience, while the Networker obtains information through personal relations. The relevance of these discussions to market knowledge acquisition of developing country-based firms is taken up in Chapter 6.

Chapter 3

Internationalization Motives
and Market Selection Decisions

This chapter discusses two key issues concerning export marketing decisions and strategy: export motives and overseas market selection decisions. The decision to go abroad is widely considered to be the critical first step in a firm's internationalization process. For most firms, this decision involves exporting; such other modes of entering foreign markets as licensing and direct production abroad are normally considered only after substantial experience has been acquired through export activities. It is generally assumed that a firm should have a motive for accepting or soliciting its first export order. The investigations reported in the literature therefore focus attention on factors that prompt the initial decision to export and have disregarded considerations about how long these factors sustain a firm's export drive. Two main aspects of the decision-making process have received significant attention:

1. Who within the firm makes the decision to go abroad?
2. Why is the decision made? Or, what are the principal factors motivating the decision?

It has generally been argued that research into export motives must reach beyond the firm as a legal entity to examine the ambitions and orientations of key decision makers in the firm. This chapter reviews some of the main perspectives and propositions that have emerged from these studies.

The discussion of export motives is followed by a review of the literature on overseas market selection. Market selection has also been presented as one of the critical decisions that international firms make, since market choice can be a major determinant of success or failure, especially in the early stages of an internationalization process. It has been argued that the nature and location of selected markets affects a firm's ability to coordinate its foreign operations and improve its global competitive position (O'Farrell and Wood, 1994). It is generally assumed in the existing literature that firms start their active export business operations by choosing the country or countries that they intend to enter, and then investigating these markets in detailing for the appropriate market segments and entry modes. The Learning Stages Theory discussed in Chapter 1 holds that systematic methods of market analysis may be adopted to back up market selection decisions only at later stages of the internationalization process when management commitment to the international activities is believed to be high.

A REVIEW OF CONTEMPORARY STUDIES ON EXPORT MOTIVES

Export motives are generally understood as those factors or considerations that encourage managers to initiate and sustain export activities or terminate them. Bilkey (1978) draws a distinction between factors that initiate exporting (stimuli) and factors that sustain an ongoing export commitment (motivators). Export stimuli may come either from sources within the firm itself (internal) or from sources outside the firm (external) or both.

Internal Export Motives

The main internal determinants widely referred to in the literature are the following:

1. The strength of *managerial aspiration* for growth and market security
2. *Management expectations* about the effect of exports on a firm's growth
3. *The level of management faith* in, and commitment to, export business

4. *Differential firm advantages* based on size, technology, and uniqueness of product
5. *Economies of scale* resulting from market expansion

The importance of these factors to export decisions is discussed by Johanson and Vahlne (1977) as well as Wiedersheim-Paul, Olson, and Welch (1978). Some empirical validations of them are provided by Cavusgil and Nevin (1981). Arguably, a firm's decision on whether to initiate export activities depends, in the final analysis, on the quality, attitude, and ambition of its managers (Bilkey and Tesar, 1977; Das, 1994). Managers' decision to commit resources to exporting derives from their expectation of positive payoffs from such investments and expenditures. These expectations in turn derive from the assessed competitive potentials of the firm and the congeniality of the export markets and operational environment (Schlegelmilch, 1986). In this regard, managers' level of market knowledge and general attitude toward risk are critical to their assessments and consequent decisions. Committed managers are, for example, found to actively seek information about overseas market opportunities through regular personal visits abroad. Through these visits, managers are also able to identify suitable distributors and thereby reduce uncertainties that discourage most firms from entering export business (McAuley, 1993).

As argued in Chapter 1, the Stages Models suggest that management commitment to internationalization increases over time with increased market knowledge and experience. It is therefore generally assumed in the literature that as firms' export experience increases, their managers gain better understanding of export mechanisms and are likely to perceive less uncertainty in their exporting activities. Thus, Cavusgil (1984b) argues that nonexporting firms and marginally active exporters tend to be more pessimistic in their evaluation of risks, costs, and profits than active exporters.

Age and Size of Firms

Since exporting firms, according to the Stages Models, were all originally domestic market oriented and are nurtured by their home markets, one is tempted to assume that they are old and have a long history prior to their entry into the international arena. This perception, however, has been refuted in a study by Cooper and Kleinschmidt (1985) who found that the older firms in their sample were more risk averse and conservative in their export orientation, preferring relatively safer neighboring markets compared to the younger firms. Since 1985, the economy has become more and more global, and consequently, more and more companies, especially small high-tech companies, are "born international."

As to resourcefulness, it is generally assumed that firm size is positively correlated to the decision to export; that is, the larger the firm, the higher the propensity to export (Cavusgil, Bilkey, and Tesar, 1979; Cavusgil and Nevin, 1981; Cavusgil and Naor, 1987). The ability of larger firms to marshall substantial resources to finance export operations has also been suggested as improving their chances for success in export markets. Taking this argument further, one is tempted to believe that managers of larger firms would have better access to market information and therefore a more rational foundation for their risk assessment and expectations. The stronger resource base would also make it easier for them to show greater commitment to export activities than smaller firms would.

Despite the volume of empirical research on the issue, no conclusive support exists for the hypothesis that firm size has a positive influence on export activity (Katsikeas and Morgan, 1994). Based on evidence from small Italian exporting firms, Bonaccorsi (1992) argues that "the amount and quality of firm resources needed for international involvement depends on the export strategy adopted and implemented" (p. 622). This implies that although smaller firms have relatively limited resources, they can enter into export business by adopting less costly approaches of market involvement. For example, firms selling nonbranded goods, whose market performance depends more on such parameters as price, delivery, and after-sales services than on brand awareness, can sell to several marginal markets using a combination of entry modes that minimizes their cost of involvement.

Economies of Scale

Assuming that all firms aim to maximize the use of their productive resources, larger firms, it is argued, will tend to seek new markets for their products to minimize their unit costs of operation and thereby improve their competitive positions and growth opportunities.

The size argument is even taken one step further by Cavusgil (1984a). He views the relationship between firm size and export activity as associative rather than causal. That is, the true relationship is between various advantages that accrue from large size rather than size itself. In this sense, larger firm size is seen as a source of differential advantage.

Corroborating evidence for the economies of scale thesis has been provided by Sullivan and Bauerschmidt's (1988) study of firms in the European forest products business. They found that "pressure to use fully capital intensive assets prompts managers to offset domestic downturns or market saturation by channelling products to overseas markets and thus maintain efficient operating rates" (p. 44). This observation, however, also indicates that such decisions may be temporary and in response to cyclical fluctuations on the domestic market. That is, firms may adopt a policy of off-loading surpluses on international markets during lean periods in domestic markets and redirecting the products to domestic buyers once that market picks up again. Foreign market involvements under such conditions would therefore be erratic and unplanned.

The economies of scale argument offers an explanation for differences in the export orientation among industries. By nature of their products or by reasons of sheer systemic influence of market leaders in a given industry, firms in a particular industry may show greater enthusiasm for exports than firms in other industries. This may be the case, for example, if the initial entrants into the industry/sector showed interest in export business from the onset and have achieved positive results from this decision. This export market orientation will influence the behavior of subsequent entrants into the industry. As will become evident from our discussion of the commercial pineapple business in Ghana, the high degree of interest shown in exports by the pineapple farmers is partly due to the export performance of the first commercial pineapple farmer in the country.

In summary, the evidence from empirical investigations of internal determinants of export decisions is not entirely conclusive. Factors such as firm size and scale of operation do not in themselves determine export decisions or performance. Considerations such as managerial aspirations, expectations, and faith in the opinions of industry and channel members regarding export opportunities may exert powerful influence on export decisions.

External Export Motives

The previous internal motives are combined with a variety of triggering cues outside the discretionary influence of individual firms to encourage firms to initiate export activities. The role of government policy has received consistent attention in the literature as one of the primary triggers of initial export decisions. Governments may initiate positive changes in the incentive structures aimed directly at stimulating export business. The most cited of these policy instruments and facilities are government-sponsored trade fairs, information about foreign market opportunities, tax incentives, and infrastructural changes designed to mitigate the negative impact on firms of perceived export barriers (Johanson and Vahlne, 1977; Wiedersheim-Paul, Olson, and Welch, 1978; Cavusgil and Nevin, 1981; Sullivan and Bauerschmidt, 1988).

Host government macroeconomic policies can also stimulate exports by increasing the trading opportunities for foreign firms. A case in point is the political economy of deregulation, privatization, and integration, which are currently vital policy matters in several countries, notably the former planned economies of Eastern Europe. Although providing immediate opportunities for foreign firms, these policies, by changing the structural features of the domestic markets, indirectly stimulate the internationalization of firms in those countries as well. For one thing, firms that experience drastic erosion of their hitherto protected domestic markets due to the entry of new competitors may react by seeking new markets elsewhere. As subsequent discussions will indicate, such firms may enter into various forms of business relations with other foreign and/or domestic firms to improve their resource base, thereby advancing their competitive positions in the new markets.

Apart from government-established export promotion institutions, information about demand and market situations in other countries may also be obtained through trade and industry associations as well as individual managers. Information that one's competitors within the domestic market are engaged in export business will doubtlessly encourage other firms in the industry to consider the possibility of doing the same. Information may also come from export agents whose business it is to visit potential exporters and encourage them to enter the international market by commissioning them to find markets for their products.

Reactive and Proactive Export Decisions and Behaviors of Firms

Export decisions are also classified in terms of whether firms respond passively to internal or external pressures, i.e., *reactive behavior,* or whether they take initiatives and act aggressively to exploit advantages that they create for themselves or are created by institutions such as the government, i.e., *proactive behavior.* Again, as discussed in Chapter 1, the Stages Models of internationalization see firms' initial involvements in foreign markets as being characterized by incremental adjustments to changing internal and external conditions rather than the result of deliberate strategies. As argued in the Stages Models, managers typically have hazy ideas about export business prior to their initial export decisions. They normally start their export experiment by responding to unsolicited orders, without any specific profit goal in mind. Some analysts attribute these initial decisions to the naive excitement of individual managers who wish to satisfy their personal idiosyncrasies. Initial marketing and organizational resource investments are typically low. But as export results prove promising, further "experiments" are undertaken, and the positive experience leads to active involvement in an increasing number of new and operationally different markets.

Although many firms proactively plan their entrance into foreign markets, most firms are likely to exhibit proactive behavior only when experimental exports prove to be lucrative over a period of time and an increasing share of their earnings come from these export ventures. They then begin to devote greater resources to market analysis and product development/modification in response to the specific needs of foreign markets.

In summary, the contemporary literature discusses export motives in terms of internal or external influences and whether the firms' responses are reactive or proactive to those influences (see Table 3.1).

TABLE 3.1. A Classification of Export Motives

Firm Behavior	Motivational Factors	
	Internal	**External**
Reactive	Risk diversification Utilization of excess capacity	Unsolicited orders Small home market Stagnant or declining home market
Proactive	Managerial urge Growth and profit goals Marketing advantages Economies of scale Unique product/technology competence	Foreign market opportunities Government export promotional efforts

Source: Albaum et al., 1994, p. 31.

SOME CRITICAL REFLECTIONS ON THE EXISTING STUDIES

A few methodological concerns must be registered about the studies on which the ideas have been based. First of all, it is worth noting that most of the studies are based on empirical data collected through questionnaires and interviews several decades after the initial decision to export was made. This approach creates inevitable difficulties. First, motives change over time and it is possible that the respondents rationalize the initial export decision in looking back several years after the decision was made. Second, several motives could underlie the initial decision, and it is difficult to say which single motive was dominant at the time the decision was made. Third, "official" and "unofficial" motives for market entry may exist. Core economic motives of sales growth and profit may compete with the personal motives and idiosyncrasies of individual managers. Furthermore, motives may vary with the market entry opportunities that exist at a given point during decision making.

The emphasis on management orientation and commitment as a foundational prerequisite for internationalization decisions has its roots in reverse deduction. Satisfactory export performance requires painstaking effort and a vast amount of development activity. Half-hearted export efforts are bound to result in failure. Successful firms are the ones whose managers approach export marketing with thorough planning combined with determination and devotion (Czinkota and Ronkainen, 1990). On its face, this argument is highly persuasive. But closely considered, one notices that it is based on the assumption that foreign market entry decisions and approaches are the result of systematic, rational considerations. Decisions motivated by sheer chance (e.g., coincidentally being at the right place at the right time) or the various arrangements that firms can make to reduce the costs of market search and entry are generally ignored in such a perception.

Furthermore, firms that may be judged at the time of empirical investigation as inactive and lacking devotion to international marketing might have been highly committed and active at the point of their initial foreign market entry decision. Their apparent inactivity may be due to changes within the organization or the negative results of initial efforts. This observation implies that longitudinal investigations are required if researchers are to expect a true understanding of the internationalization decisions and processes of the firms they investigate.

It is also generally acknowledged in mainstream literature that as firms increase their level of international involvement, they tend to change their methods of operation and the structure of their organizations in response to the increasing complexity of their activities. The discussion of export motives appears, however, to be limited to the initial decision to export. Appropriate questions to ask are, "How long do initial export motives persist?" "When do new motives emerge?" and "What considerations bring about changes in export motives?" It seems quite obvious that the driving motives at the initiation point of internationalization will not persist when international operations form an ordinary and accepted part of the firm's activities. Studies are therefore required to inform us on the changes and their influence on strategies.

INTERNATIONAL MARKET SELECTION DECISIONS

As noted earlier, export decisions are immediately followed by decisions on which markets to target for sales. The literature on export market selection examines how the selection decisions are made. Issues examined include whether the decisions are deliberate and planned, i.e., whether the firms engage in systematic analysis as a basis for their decisions, or whether the decision-making process is considerably unsystematic and coincidental. The discussions in this section will draw attention to the relevance of such factors as market similarity, market size, product characteristics, geographic proximity, cultural distance, country risk, and intensity of competition for the choice of markets for firms in developing countries.

Conventional Approaches to Market Selection

Going back to the internationalization process discussed in the Stages Models, it can be argued that deliberate market selection enters the decision frame of firms that take exporting seriously and are willing to commit resources to market searches i.e., firms at Stages 3 through 6 (see Table 1.2 in Chapter 1). Two alternative approaches to market selection have been suggested: *the expansive approach* and *the contractible approach*. Firms adopting the expansive approach move gradually and incrementally into the international market, starting from markets that are geographically close and culturally similar to the domestic market. The contractible approach involves a systematic filtering of the global market using a set of criteria to arrive at a market considered most suitable for the firm. Once a country has been identified as a suitable export market, the selection task is focused on analysis of the different relevant market segments in the country and a choice of one or several segments that are most likely to help the firm fulfill its export objectives. The two dominant approaches are discussed in detail in the following material.

The Expansive Approach

The view that exporting begins with geographically close and culturally similar markets and extends sequentially to more distant countries has won general acceptance in the international business literature, drawing its validation from some published empirical evidence (Cundiff and Hilger, 1988; Albaum et al., 1994; Hollensen, 1998). The general view is that similarities reduce managers' perceived risk in entering the market and, for that matter, the amount of information required for them to make a final decision.

Geographic proximity of the foreign market has been noted to be positively correlated to market similarity, since it increases the probability of the two countries sharing cultural values and approaches to business. With a lower cultural distance, the exporting firm can more confidently transfer familiar marketing methods and techniques to the new market. Marketing personnel can also operate in the new environment with less difficulty. The net result is that the overall costs of operating in similar markets are lower than in unfamiliar markets. SMEs have therefore been noted to show high preference for geographically close and culturally similar markets, particularly during the initial stages of their internationalization processes (Johanson and Vahlne, 1977; Cavusgil, Bilkey, and Tesar, 1979; Strandskov, 1987).

It has been observed that firms with established positions in a particular market tend to show reluctance to move into new, unfamiliar markets if opportunities exist for them to expand their operations in the familiar markets. Decisions to venture into unknown markets are made only if the relative payoffs are greater in the new markets, perhaps due to a unique differential advantage possessed by the firms, such as product differentiation that provides superior value to consumers in those particular markets (O'Farrell and Wood, 1994).

Although the near-market approach is logically defensible, Cooper and Kleinschmidt (1985) indicate in their study that it is not a strong determinant of export success. In fact, the distant-market-oriented firms in their sample clearly and consistently outperformed their nearest-neighbor counterparts. They describe the highest export performers in their sample as follows: "aggressive and entrepreneurial firms; young and with few years of export experience; heavy R&D [research and development] spending but no product price advantage; extensive export planning; and high export expectations" (Cooper and Kleinschmidt, 1985, p. 48).

The Contractible Approach

Whereas the expansive approach to market selection is based on innate knowledge and experience, the contractible approach assumes analytical capacity, i.e., systematic screening of markets based on an agreed-upon set of selection criteria (cf the Planning Man approach discussed in Chapter 2). The starting point is the totality of world markets that, through a rational screening procedure, is gradually reduced to a few markets assessed to be the most attractive for a firm's products.

The preliminary screening tries to minimize two errors: the error of ignoring countries that offer good prospects for a firm's product type and the error of spending too much time investigating countries that are poor prospects (Root, 1987). Consequently, the chosen screening criteria are broad in nature and depend largely on available secondary data, such as physical and geographic features of the countries as well as macrosocioeconomic, demographic, political, and legal information.

This helps the company to assess, in broad terms, the extent to which these markets can enable it to attain its overall objectives. After the number of markets has been reduced to a more manageable level, the market analyst will then collect more detailed information on a market-by-market basis for a preliminary evaluation. The information helps the analyst to determine the fastest growing markets among the group of markets considered for a particular product as well as market trends and market restrictions. Issues such as social habits, local tastes, and preferences of the range of products within the industry, as well as their demand patterns, are examined.

This is followed by collection and analysis of information about existing and potential competition, ease of market entry, cost of entry, and estimated profit potentials of the products in question. The understanding is that countries which pass this screening have a high likelihood of being profitable. The last stage of the screening, therefore, focuses on the selected countries and engages in a detailed analysis of how the firm can enter these markets and which factors may affect implementation of marketing plans and strategies.

The general understanding is that a firm's size and its degree of internationalization will affect the extent to which it uses systematic methods of market selection. A large and highly international firm may prefer to use more elaborate market selection procedures than its smaller and domestically based counterpart. Furthermore, firms may strategically choose to concentrate their marketing efforts on certain key markets and ignore others at specific stages in their internationalization processes.

Despite the profound academic faith in systematic information collection and screening of markets, the available empirical evidence suggests that the use of this approach is not as widespread as would be expected. At a general level, Keegan (1974) discovered, in an empirical study of American international business managers, that the most frequent sources of information are personal contacts and staff members in the firms' international subsidiaries. Rarely did managers use market research or publications of any kind as sources of information. Permut (1977) also concluded, from a study of European business executives' use of market research, that the development of more sophisticated techniques seemed far less important to executives than having action-oriented sources of information on which they could rely.

These findings are consistent with the results of Cavusgil's (1984b) study of modes of market selection by international marketing executives from seventy American companies. Cavusgil noted in that study that the executives typically adopted less rigorous, less formal, and less quantitative approaches to international market information collection than was the case when investigating domestic markets. A rigorous quantitative analysis of the international marketing data, if collected, and a rank ordering of foreign markets in terms of the opportunities they offer were the exception rather than the rule. Consistent with the evidence in Keegan's (1974) study, many of the executives in Cavusgil's study identified travel or personal contacts as their most valuable and reliable sources of overseas information. Holbert (1974) made similar observations. Furthermore, studies have indicated that no major differences exist between users and nonusers of international market research, particularly with respect to their perception of export obstacles (Diamantopuolos, Schlegelmilch, and Allpress, 1990). These general observations have been corroborated in more recent writings (McAuley, 1993; Eriksson et al., 1997).

Externally Created/Prescribed Markets

External stimuli, such as bilateral agreements between governments and government-sponsored trade delegations to foreign countries, may also create market opportunities for selected firms in a given country or bring such opportunities to the notice of firms. Firms in this kind of situation may be said to choose their markets opportunistically. In other words, although the companies are alert to new opportunities, the search and market identification activities are rather random or casual. This observation is consistent with the expectations of the internationalization process of firms described in the Stages Models. Due to limited resources or their limited involvement in export, firms whose market selection is triggered by external influences may stick to only those markets where some prospect of selling remains. They are not likely to make deliberate efforts to find other markets.

The two most common means by which foreign market opportunities are deliberately fostered through external intervention are:

1. bilateral political arrangements
2. trade promotions

The first type of initiative includes barter trade agreements between nations that exchange goods and resources among themselves. Examples of such agreements are Ghana's exchange of salt for beef with Mali and its exchange of tropical fruit juice for petroleum from Libya. Such political agreements offer opportunities for firms dealing with the products in the respective countries to engage in export to specific countries with which the agreements have been signed. It is normal for the political institutions concerned with the implementation of the agreements to be accorded the mandates to select local firms that will undertake the exporting and distribution of the goods.

The political arrangement can also be formulated within the framework of bilateral aid aimed at supporting the development of specific economic activities or infrastructure in a specific country. These forms of agreements are normally between the developed economies on the one side and the developing and/or transitional economies on the other.

These agreements offer opportunities for firms in the donor countries to export technology and related services to the aid recipient countries or to engage in joint ventures or other forms of business alliances with firms in the developing and transitional economies. An example of this form of political market arrangement is the private sector program initiated by Danish International Development Assistance (DANIDA) in six developing countries (Ghana, Zimbabwe, Egypt, Uganda, Vietnam, and India) that are among the major recipients of Danish development assistance.[1]

Apart from these arrangements, a country can deliberately pursue aggressive export growth strategies by attending local trade exhibitions and fairs or by supporting participational arrangements abroad. The objective of trade fair participation is to expose firms and their products to potential customers. The trade promotion institutions may purposefully select exhibitions and fairs in which they would like the firms in their countries to participate. The selection may be based on their assessment of how promising a particular country's market is for the key export products they would like to promote. In this way, the market selection decisions are partly in the hands of the trade promotion institutions. As the empirical evidence from Ghana will show (see Chapter 10), many of the country's exporters of nontraditional products have based their market selection decisions on contracts and information acquired through participation in trade fairs or by fulfilling orders passed on to them through the export promotion institutions in the country.

Regionalization and Market Selection

Regional trade agreements and economic as well as political integration have become significant instruments by which cross-border market opportunities are created in the world economy. Today, the most successful example of such an economic integration experiment is the European Union. Similar experiments do exist, for example, the Association of Southeast Asian Nations (ASEAN) and the North American Free Trade Agreement (NAFTA). In their crudest form such agreements reduce or eliminate tariff and nontariff barriers among the member states and thereby encourage the mobility of goods, services, and factors of production. Thus, the temptation of firms to target markets within a specific economic block of which their countries are members is very high.

Seen in this light, the Economic Community of West African States (ECOWAS), established in 1975, should provide Ghanaian firms with an opportunity to export their products to other West African markets.

History-Based Market Selection

For firms in some countries, previous political links to certain countries may offer them special opportunities for targeting those markets. The U.K. market is a classic example that illustrates the importance of historical and political links for market selection. Empirical evidence has shown that firms from most African countries are former British colonies look for customers for their products mainly in the United Kingdom (Jaffee, 1993). The reason may be that the U.K. market is familiar to businesspeople from these countries, possibly through previous sojourns in the United Kingdom.

Furthermore, it is possible that many U.K. trading companies still have subsidiaries and agencies in their former colonies and therefore are members of the local business communities. To the extent that inexperienced exporters rely on these networks and relations, one would expect the U.K. agents and sales representatives to have a strong influence on the local businesspeople's international market knowledge. The systematic impact of such market selection decisions cannot be underestimated in the developing countries.

The empirical investigation reported in this book will seek to assess the extent to which the historical factor has impacted on the market selection decisions of Ghanaian firms.

Other Views on Market Selection

The previous discussions suggest that the expansive-contractible dichotomy provides just a rudimentary approximation of the options available to firms in their choice of export markets. Compiling empirical evidence from various studies, including the authors' own, the following modifications and alternatives to the expansive and contractible approaches to market selection can be offered:

1. Unsolicited orders from foreign agents or importers
2. Alertness and passive search
3. Niche market search

These three approaches are consistent with the views expressed in Chapter 2 in regard to market knowledge acquisition, with particular reference to the behavior of the Action Man and the Networker.

Unsolicited Orders

Available empirical evidence indicates that many firms initiate their entry into the export business by fulfilling unsolicited orders from importers hitherto unknown to them (Cavusgil and Nevin, 1981; Strandskov, 1987). If the importer proves reliable and places frequent orders, that importer becomes a key customer of the firm and a relationship develops between them. Thus, by agreeing to fill orders placed by the importer/customer, the exporting firm indirectly makes a market choice. The relationship may prove enduring or may collapse subject to the turn of events and the degree of trust and mutual benefits it provides the parties. The exporter may opt out of markets where the relationship with original importers could not be sustained or find substitute channel members to maintain presence in the market if such arrangements prove feasible.

Alertness

Earlier studies, particularly those underlying the Stages Models, perceive firms' initial responses to orders from importers as evidence of passivity and noncommitment to exporting. The generalizability of such a perception is questionable. As discussed earlier, a prospective exporting firm may be engaged in a conscious search for opportunities to sell abroad, without necessarily performing elaborate market screening or market research. It may, for example, seek markets by registering in trade directories and with export promotion institutions in its country in the hope that it will be linked with serious importers/agents abroad. In anticipation of the results of the empirical analysis (see Part II), we argue that many leading exporting firms in developing countries may initiate their entry into the export business through such arrangements. This is a legitimate proactive strategy for resource-poor firms that see this approach as the only realistic initial market search strategy.

Niche Market Search

In other situations, the market search effort may not proceed as described in the screening model. One such situation is when the prospective exporter produces goods and/or services earmarked for limited users in a few markets/countries. Sales of specialized equipment for space programs are one example; specialized consultancy services for major projects are another example. In such situations, potential customers can be readily identified and direct contacts made without any elaborate search or macroeconomic analysis.

In summary, it can be argued that a company's choice of market selection approach depends upon such contextual features as size, nature of products, number of potential customers, and industry traditions. Most developing country-based firms are likely to show limited preference for elaborate screening models partly because their volumes of production do not warrant a search for big markets. Sheer alertness and simple information searches through business colleagues may be adequate for such companies to identify reliable channel members in a few markets to sell their products. For such companies, choice of a distributor or an agent is therefore an important first step toward market choice.

SUMMARY

Two issues of critical importance to the internationalization process of firms were discussed in this chapter. First, we examined the literature on factors triggering firms' initial export decisions. The prevailing understanding is that four sets of motives may underlie managers' decisions to embark on the exportation of their firms' products: (1) proactive internal motives, (2) proactive external motives, (3) reactive internal motives, and (4) reactive external motives (see Table 3.1). The decision to go abroad naturally enjoins managers to select overseas markets that will fulfill their corporate objectives. Two broad approaches to market selection are suggested in the literature: (1) the expansive approach, which follows the prescriptions of the Stages Models, and (2) the contractible approach, which assumes that firms undertake systematic market data collection and analysis as a basis of screening potential markets to arrive at the best market. As with the other issues discussed in the available literature on export marketing, the ideas presented are based on studies of firms located in the developed market economies. Their relevance to developing country firms is discussed in Chapter 6.

Chapter 4

Choice of Entry Mode and Organization of International Operations

The market entry and development mode is one of the three main decision variables for internationalizing firms, the other two being the choice of markets and the decision on what product/service to sell or produce abroad.[1]

A market entry and development mode is defined as the institutional/organizational arrangement established to reach and cooperate with foreign customers. The choice of market entry mode is important for three reasons:

1. Many entry modes require capital outlays and investments of some magnitude, e.g., the establishment of a sales subsidiary.
2. It takes time to build solid and durable relations with foreign partners, and when established, a change of entry mode (e.g., moving from an importer to a wholly owned sales subsidiary) may entail substantial additional investments. Such a change may also damage the exporter's reputation.
3. Establishing an entry mode is not just a simple marketing issue; it involves organizational and cross-cultural management issues as well, e.g., when cooperating with an importer or, more so, when establishing a strategic alliance.

THEORIES OF MARKET ENTRY AND DEVELOPMENT MODES

Figure 4.1 provides an overview of the various market entry modes that have been discussed in international business literature. The following are the three main categories:

1. Export/import, i.e., trading modes (transaction modes)
2. Cooperation/coalition modes (transfer modes)
3. Foreign direct investment (FDI) modes (transformation modes)

Historically, theories of trade with David Ricardo's concept of national comparative advantages based on differences in labor productivity as their starting point have dominated the literature. Following this theory, a country is said to have comparative advantage whenever the *relative* ability of that country to produce a particular product differs from those of other countries. Countries should

FIGURE 4.1. Alternative Foreign Market Entry Modes

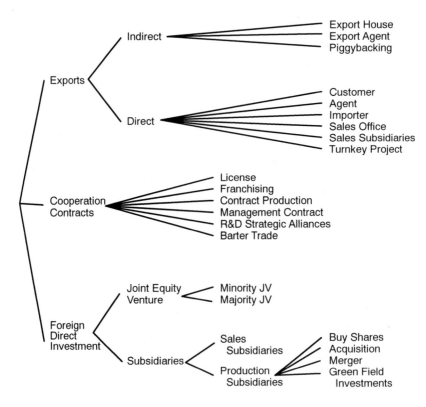

Source: Adapted from Sørensen, 1996a.

therefore specialize in producing products for which they enjoy the greatest *relative* advantage (or the *relatively* least disadvantage), as measured in terms of relative prices. As Toyne and Walters (1989) explain, a country's comparative advantage depends on (1) the productivity of available factor inputs, principally land, labor, and capital; (2) the costs of these inputs in terms of the local currency; and (3) the prevailing foreign exchange rate during a given period. Changes in any of these variables will have important implications for a country's comparative advantage.

In the early postwar period, FDI theories started emerging as a separate discipline because FDIs were incompatible with mainstream thinking within trade theories. In recent years, FDI theories (coalitions, strategic alliances, partnerships, etc.) have received increasing attention, both in the literature and in practice. Of these theories, the following are of particular relevance to this chapter's discussion of market entry modes:

- The Learning Stages Theory of company internationalization and the International Product Life Cycle Theory focus on the changes in market entry/development modes over time.
- The Transaction Costs Theory and the Eclectic Paradigm focus on the conditions for choosing the market (exports) or the hierarchy (investments abroad) at any point in time, i.e., to externalize or internalize the international operations.
- The Network Theory focuses on the building of network relations across borders, given the degree of internationalization of the industry and the company in question.
- Finally, the Theory of Strategic Alliances, together with the Network Theory, forms part of the new scientific growth area. The theory is in its infancy, struggling with legitimizing coalitions as a third independent governance structure in addition to the market and the hierarchy (Young et al., 1989, p. 29; Powell, 1991; Håkansson and Johanson, 1993).

The contributions made by each of the theories to the understanding of the internationalization of companies in general were presented in Chapter 1; readers are referred to this account for an overview of the theories. The focus in the remainder of this chapter is on how the theories deal with market entry and development modes.

CHOOSING MARKET ENTRY
AND DEVELOPMENT MODES

The three interrelated key issues a firm may have to deal with are

1. the choice of entry mode when entering a new market,
2. the change in entry mode when the firm gradually internationalizes, and
3. the management of a portfolio of market entry and development modes.

Choice of Market Entry Modes

Empirically, the following six ways of deciding which market
entry mode to select have been identified (Sørensen, 1996a).

Choice According to Industry Tradition

Business norms exist in many, especially mature, industries. New
entrants into these industries are expected to obey the rules to gain a
position. Thus, the problem for the newcomer is not which entry
mode to choose (the past has already made that decision); it is how
to penetrate the often tightly structured market. African cut-flower
exporters' experience in Europe provides an illustration of this
point. Since the European cut-flower market is highly concentrated
and most customers buy their cut-flowers from the Dutch flower
auction, it has been extremely difficult for the small, inexperienced
African exporters to penetrate the markets.

The Unsolicited or Reactive Choice

As already indicated, many companies are motivated to go international by filling unsolicited orders. By doing so, they implicitly or
explicitly acknowledge the importer as their representative abroad.
Theoretically, this decision mode will normally be categorized as
"irrational." Considering, however, the scope of the world and how
impossible it is to foresee and plan everything, one may also perceive the situation more positively as "an expected but unpredict-

able opportunity" that a company can exploit successfully if it has the necessary action capacity.

The Predetermined Choice of Entry Mode

As stipulated in the Stages Models of internationalization (Chapter 1), empirical studies have revealed a certain pattern in the internationalization of companies. That is, a company moves from one mode to another in a sequential and orderly manner. For market entry and development modes, the stereotypical pattern is illustrated in Figure 4.2.

The pattern indicates that, over time, companies increase their commitment (and hence financial risks) as they increase their control over market activities. To the extent that the pattern is valid, the critical issue for a company is not which entry mode to choose but when to change the entry mode.

The Contingency Choice

Empirically, the Learning Stages Theory of internationalization is under heavy attack. Many claim that the uniqueness of each market at any point in time, together with the exporter's resources and strategy, forms the basis for the decision on market entry mode. In other words, the entry mode decision is contingent on the specific circumstances.

Thus, all options are open, and the company analyst and the planner will have to join forces to identify decision criteria and

FIGURE 4.2. Choices of Entry Mode According to the Stages Models

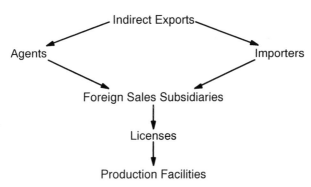

analytical tools to provide the decision maker with an assessment of the alternative entry modes.

The criteria used for the choice of market entry and development mode will be company specific. However, the most commonly used criteria are

- financial risks involved by using a specific mode,
- control over market activities, and
- cost efficiency.

In addition to these, a company may also consider

- reversibility and/or exit costs and
- feedback from the market, i.e., learning effects.

Table 4.1 provides a framework for choosing among the most commonly employed operational modes, using financial risk and marketing control as the decision criteria.

Underlying the contingency choice is the Planning Man approach (see Chapter 2). The limitations of this approach are caused by the presence of uncertainty, related especially to international (volatile) markets, and the bounded rationality of the analyst, the planner, and the decision maker.

TABLE 4.1. Control/Risk Matrix for the Choice of International Market Entry Mode

Degree of Control	Financial Risks		
	Low	Medium	High
Low	Acting as a subcontractor Sales to local export company	Overseas distributor/importer	
Medium	Foreign agent Licensing	Franchising	Joint venture
High			Sales Production subsidiary

The Evolutionary and Network Choice

In practice, an entry mode is often chosen, not unsolicited and not following comprehensive planning, but based on the extension of existing networks of which the potential exporter is a member. That is, the new foreign partners are identified using the existing network, which serves as the springboard for new foreign ventures. It may be as simple as the company supplier having a contact abroad that can be approached, or an existing foreign customer in one country having contacts to some colleagues in one or several other countries.

The advantage of using the present network as a base for choosing new foreign partners is that the partners know one another well. The trust and mutual orientation that they have established from long-term cooperation will enable firms within the network to work toward the attainment of one another's needs. Furthermore, using the network approach to choose entry modes reduces the costs of searching for new partners as well as the risks of choosing the wrong partner.

The Strategic Choice

As part of overall corporate planning, the strategic choice of entry modes aims to establish, maintain, and develop a viable fit between the organizational motives, objectives, and resources and the changing market opportunities (Young et al., 1989, p. 36).

Choosing entry modes according to the strategic choice model involves elements of, but goes beyond, the rational planning and cost minimization issues included in the contingency approach. For example, the strategic decision mode takes into account and anticipates reactions from rivals, or it aims to be present in a market to ensure access to knowledge and other resources. In other words, the strategic choice mode does not have the clarity and rigidity of the contingency approach. It is a pragmatic approach to decision making that subjectively weighs internal and external factors against each other. Rigid analytical tools from the contingency analytic tool kit may, however, be used as an integrated part of the strategic choice mode.

Depending on the company's approach to corporate planning, entry modes may be chosen according to the strategic planning or the strategic management approach. The difference between the two is that the former is suited to situations with relatively low complexity and a stable environment, whereas the strategic management approach is geared toward situations characterized by complexity, uncertainty, and diversity—a situation often facing the exporter.

Strategic management aims at being able to exploit the many unexpected opportunities that arise in export marketing. As such, it involves continuous monitoring of the markets, reparation of discrete scenarios of the future, building of "excess" financial and managerial capacity, companywide strategy discussions and formulations, and the building of implementation and action capacity. Thus, strategic management makes the company reactive in a proactive manner.

Changing Operational Modes and Managing a Portfolio of Entry Modes

Over time, a company may have or want to change from the original market entry mode to another way of servicing the foreign market in which it operates. Such changes are often very complicated because they involve the reshuffling of people.

A simpler case occurs when a company realizes that it has made a bad choice and thus needs to replace one agent or importer with another. The more complicated case occurs when a market grows and the company wants to switch to a mode with higher company commitment and control over the market activities, e.g., from an agent to a sales subsidiary.

Basically, the previous six decision modes can be used for changing a decision just as they are used to make the initial decision. The unsolicited choice mode may be used because, suddenly, an importer goes broke. In case the company wants to shift, for example, from an agent to a sales subsidiary because the market has grown, it may, so as not to lose valuable market knowledge, offer the agent the position of manager of the subsidiary.

Apart from the problem of shifting from one mode to another, international companies often have to manage a portfolio of entry modes. For example, a company may use agents in secondary markets while importers or sales subsidiaries serve primary markets.

The company may also have licensed contracts and perhaps even a production subsidiary or joint venture.

The exact composition of the portfolio of entry modes thus depends on the importance of the markets served and the amount of time the company has operated in the market. Often, it also depends on governmental policies within each of the markets. Maybe only licensed or joint ventures are allowed, while imports as well as fully owned production subsidiaries are prohibited.

When a company uses different entry modes, the choice becomes more complicated. In principle, the optimal choice is made for each market. However, economies of scale, learning curves, synergies, etc., may make it more feasible to concentrate on certain types of market servicing modes.

SUMMARY

This chapter provided an overview of the various alternative entry strategies at the disposal of an international company. Attention was focused on the factors that influence managers' choice of entry modes at three stages: (1) the initial stages of their internationalization processes, (2) when their degrees of internationalization increase and the need for changes in entry modes is felt, and (3) at stages of deeper commitment and involvement in the internationalization process, requiring the management of a portfolio of market entry and development modes. Within each of these situations, managers must consciously assess the relative payoffs of the alternative choices and the long-term implications of their choices for the overall direction and effectiveness of their internationalization processes.

Chapter 5

Relationships and Interaction Within the Domestic Economy and Across Borders

The notion that business systems are socially embedded is now gaining acceptance in the economic literature (Whitley, 1994). Attention is increasingly focused on market actors who reach major business agreements through personal contacts and handshakes. Written contracts tend to assume a secondary importance in business relations today.

Furthermore, empirical studies have revealed (Kuada and Sørensen, 1997) that managers often base their decisions on the advice of a few personal and trustworthy informants rather than on research reports. Similarly, the internationalization of firms is often based on the establishment of personal contacts overseas. In fact, exporters often state that they rely solely on personal visits to a market or personal contacts to promote their business. Comprehensive market studies cannot replace such personal acquaintances.

Thus, for the business manager, the market is not composed of anonymous factors and forces. It is "real" in the sense that it includes identifiable, autonomous actors/people with whom long-term relations can be established.

The importance of personal relations, networks, etc., has grown in recent years due to increased use of international out-sourcing. The trend toward increasing information, knowledge, and technology flows has also contributed to the growing importance of relationships. Examples of economic organization modes based primarily on personal relations are strategic alliances and the lean production system. (Michalet, 1991; Gundlach, Achrol, and Mentzer, 1995; Dunning, 1995).

THEORIES OF RELATIONSHIPS
AND INTERACTION

In the last ten to twenty years, the "social-organizational" dimension of business (in contrast to the transactional perspective) has drawn a lot of research attention and may be considered as an alternative approach to understanding business, in general, and the internationalization of firms, in particular. The new dimension has emerged under different headings: theories of relationships, interaction, interfirm links, partnerships, strategic alliances, etc.

Many researchers with different scientific perspectives have contributed to the debate. Notable among them are researchers from Uppsala University who have produced a conceptual framework that they call the network approach (Johanson and Mattsson, 1988). Along the same lines, Morgan and Hunt (1994, p. 20) suggest the term "network paradigm" to distinguish this approach to studying business activities from conventional approaches. In explaining relationship marketing, Morgan and Hunt (1994) distinguish between "discrete transactions," which are normally of short duration, and "relational exchanges," which are of longer duration (p. 21). To them, relationship marketing embraces all activities aimed at the initiation and sustenance of successful "relational exchanges" (p. 22). They further argue that successful relational exchanges depend on commitment and trust between the collaborating firms. "Relationship marketing" is expected to be the dominant approach to marketing in the future. In the words of Gundlach, Achrol, and Mentzer (1995), "the marketing discipline moves further away from the transactional view of exchange and embraces the relational view" (pp. 78-79).

Key concepts in relationship marketing are trust and commitment, and by basing exchange on long-term relations, it is possible for the company to cope with uncertainties, bounded rationality, and opportunism while close interaction promotes innovative activities.

In sum, interfirm coalitions are growing. A theory of relationships and interaction is emerging through numerous contributions from a variety of scientific fields.[1] Relationship theory and its relevance to the internationalization of enterprises will be dealt with in four areas:

1. The Network Theory, focusing especially on the Uppsala version discussed previously (Johanson and Mattsson, 1988).

2. Cross-border strategic alliances will be presented and discussed, focusing on alliances between SMEs in different countries (Sørensen and Kuada, 1998b).
3. A Partnership Model will be presented to discuss the relationship between government and the business community, focusing on the promotion of exports and FDI (Sørensen, 1994b).
4. The Theory of Industrial Districts (clusters) will be presented to discuss how relations/proximity within local industrial centers may foster competitive advantages that can be exploited internationally (Porter, 1990, 1994; Schmitz and Musyck, 1994).

The following discussions are aimed at providing an overview of the roles of strategic alliances, business-government relations, and industrial clusters in the internationalization process of firms.

Strategic Alliances (SAs)

A strategic alliance entails voluntary, collaborative agreements between companies. The main purposes of an SA are (1) to get access to resources controlled by the partner, (2) to share risks, and (3) to share benefits. In principle, no equity investments are involved, although many authors include joint equity ventures/ownership in the group of strategic alliances. Examples of strategic alliances are R&D cooperation, licenses, franchising, subcontracting, management contracts, technical assistance contracts, etc.

Strategic alliances as an international market entry mode have been on the increase in the last ten years (Faulkner, 1995). This increase can be explained as follows:

1. Firms become more specialized and begin to concentrate on a core competency.
2. This leads to more important innovations and an accelerated commercialization of these products are to gain competitive advantage.
3. Thus, the integration of a multitude of different kinds of technologies from a wide range of disciplines becomes more important, and strategic alliances become more relevant to the firms.

Presently, firms outsource marginal activities and support services in order to concentrate on a core business, to attain economies of scale, often on a worldwide platform, and to be in the forefront technologically. Today, innovations and their commercial exploitation are the key competitive parameters in most industries. Speed and costs of R&D are crucial here, and the pooling of resources/competence is a way to overcome both.

Innovation also has a qualitative dimension: "Innovation increasingly depends on combining incremental technological advances across a wide range of disciplines" (Dunning, 1993b, p. 201). The diversity of technological development creates a potential for developing products and processes based on an integration of a portfolio of technologies. Thus, the SA's following attributes allow it to overcome organizational deficiencies and market failures:

- The SA is a fund-raising modality.
- The financial risk of R&D is shared within an SA.
- The SA overcomes some of the problems of acquiring technical and management knowledge through the market system.
- The SA fulfills the need for expedience in combining different technologies embedded in different firms and institutions (compared to internalization) as well as the need for quick entry into foreign markets.
- The SAs can be flexible in the sense of having limited duration and being relatively easy to create (although not always easy to manage).

Although SAs have flourished, especially within R&D activities among multinational enterprises (MNEs), they have also been formed within marketing, supplies, and production and among SMEs themselves or between SMEs and MNCs. In addition, the development of the private sectors in developing countries and economies in transition has created an SA potential between firms in developed and developing countries aimed at transferring know-how to former state enterprises and newly established private companies.

The Relationship Between the Business Community and the Government

The theories of government-business relations (GBR) have been dominated by the neoclassical paradigm within economics and the structure-conduct-performance paradigm from the field of industrial organization (Ferguson and Ferguson, 1994) Based on this paradigm, governments have been advised on "how to manage a market economy."

However, the soundness of the available advice remains doubtful, considering the impressive success achieved by the newly industrialized countries (NICs) in the world market. Contrary to the dominant advice from the academic literature, the NIC approach to economic development allows for active and integrative government intervention in NIC market economies. Thus, a key question in the current debate is whether market economies in development or in transition should be managed in the same way as mature market economies. Five approaches to the management of market economies have been identified (Sørensen, 1994a). They are summarized in Table 5.1.

TABLE 5.1. Roles and Models of Government in a Market Economy

Type of Government	Public Authority (Public Sector)	Private Autonomy (Private Sector)
Laissez-Faire	Minimize	Maximize
Mixed Economy	Division of labor between government and private sector based on effectiveness and efficiency.	
Partnership Model	Dialogue between government and private sector. The dialogue takes place within a network of public and private institutions.	
Public Policy Supremacy Model	The government represents unified political power and shapes or directs the actions of private business through policies.	
Central Planning	Maximize	Minimize

Source: Sørensen, 1994b, p. 10.

In most textbooks and studies of the internationalization of companies, the government is treated as superior to the business community. The government defines the general framework within which companies operate. Therefore, no real link exists between the two parties. The same can be said about models based on division of labor. In these models, a given set of tasks is divided between the public and the private sectors on the basis of relative competence and task performance capacities. Much of the present debate in developing countries centers around this issue, including how to generate resources for the provision of, for example, physical infrastructure.

The Partnership Model, on the other hand, takes the stand that GBR must be based on cooperation and dialogue embedded in permanent public and private institutions. The institutions have various roles: initiation of debates, formulation of policies, resolution of conflicts, and monitoring of companies. The roles may be within one institution, but normally a set of institutions exists, forming a multi-centered power structure that is loosely coordinated by overall policies and directives.

This general understanding of GBR can be used to study, for example, the effectiveness of export and investment promotion schemes. By identifying barriers to international activities, the institutional arrangement can be assessed as to its ability to overcome those barriers. The framework may also be used to assess the atmosphere of collaboration between the private and public sectors. This may be done by examining their mechanisms of interaction and coordination of their respective efforts.

Relations Within Industrial Districts As a Source of International Competitive Advantage

There is an emerging understanding in the available literature that nations—or even localities within nations—form the basis for creating international competitive advantage. Related to this is the observation that MNCs have become so footloose that they source inputs and access markets at will anywhere in the world. One of the main contributors to this understanding is Porter (1994), who strongly argues that "locality" matters in the discussion of competitive advantages of firms. It is true that MNCs source inputs and access markets globally in a search for what is referred to as "static efficiency," i.e., low input costs and access to stable markets for specific products. However, the competitive advantage derived from static efficiency is of a temporal nature and, in general, is on the decline due to the globalization of markets and competition.

Since Prahalad and Hamel (1990) published their seminal article on core competencies of firms, management scholars have accepted the view that competitive advantages of firms are innovation driven rather than scale driven. That is, firms' superior performance depends largely on their ability to continuously innovate by applying their core competencies.

Firms may tend to be footloose in order to reap the benefits of static efficiency. However, dynamic improvements in their operations depend on proximity to other firms (Porter, 1994), i.e., their location within an industrial district (Schmitz and Musyck, 1994). Proximity enables firms to leverage resources and to concentrate on core competence development.

To support the proximity theory, it can be observed empirically that some companies, some localities within nations, and some nations are more competitive than others. The interesting question, however, is whether the competitive advantages are based on static efficiency of temporal character or dynamic improvement.

Many developing countries have based their promotion of foreign investments in their countries on the exploitation of static efficiency, whether in general (low input costs, tax havens, etc.) or in the form of special zones, such as export-processing zones (EPZs), free-trade zones (FTZs), or special economic zones (SEZs), as found in China. (Young et al., 1989, pp. 175-178).

Basically, developing countries have used the theory of comparative advantage as their policy guideline. However, as previously stated, such advantages may be eroded in today's global economy; other countries, through appropriate policy instruments, can easily copy the static efficiencies, and global companies have developed flexible production modes, including sourcing modes, that make it relatively easy to relocate production.

In addition, the key question today is not country-based comparative advantage but the ability on the part of the institutions in the country (firms, public agencies, business associations, research institutes, etc.) to transform the public comparative advantage into private (internationally) competitive advantage (Sørensen and Christensen, 1993). Thus, a theory of proximity, or industrial districts, to use the conventional term, is needed. Such a theory has five main elements:

1. A theory of proximity is a theory of the dynamic relationship and interaction between autonomous but interdependent enterprises and institutions based in the same locality.[2]
2. The relationships involve knowledge generation and the diffusion and application of the generated know-how to accomplish dynamic improvements. Classical deals at arm's length exist, but they do not form the crucial core of an industrial district.
3. The units constituting and interacting within an industrial district are many, with diverse qualities and capabilities: enterprises linked vertically, horizontally, and diagonally, i.e., support companies and institutions (Sørensen, 1994a); public institutions and agencies; various business associations and professional clubs; research institutions; and personal friends from whom advice is acquired.
4. A knowledge-generating relationship (rather than a purely economically based relationship) cannot be planned and established in the short term. Industrial districts evolve over time through the daily interaction among the actors making up the districts. Thus, an industrial district cannot be created or studied using simple cause-and-effect rationales. Public agencies can support the process in various ways, e.g., by providing training facilities, but they cannot direct it.
5. The industrial district encompasses both cooperation and competition. The firms cooperate to create and apply new ideas, and they compete as to who can create the best ideas. The cooperative/competitive spirit is encouraged by the fact that the industrial district has a common interest in promoting improvements to gain competitive advantage internationally.

Porter (1994) identifies the following conditions for the emergence of a dynamic industrial district:

1. Availability of specialized resources necessary for the operations of the firms
2. High customer demand for the products

3. Availability of local suppliers with specialized equipment and resources to fulfill the inputs requirements of the firms
4. The presence of locally based competitors to stimulate innovation and process improvements in the firms within the industrial district

In his view, all these conditions interact in a mutually reinforcing manner. It is therefore difficult to determine casual relationships between them.

Whereas Porter is concerned with high-tech industrial districts, or clusters, as he terms them, Schmitz and Musyck (1994) have summarized the European experience with low-tech industrial districts composed of SMEs. According to them, the main attributes of an industrial district are as follows:

1. Close geographical locations of SMEs
2. Close collaboration between firms in specialized sectors
3. Competition based on innovation rather than conditions of static efficiency
4. Sociocultural identity among firms and employees
5. The existence of self-help associations formed within the ambient civil society
6. Active regional and municipal authorities

To summarize, unlike conventional export zones with their enclave companies exploiting static efficiency, especially low labor costs, industrial districts aim to foster dynamic improvements, i.e., innovations, expansions, and internationalization. Industrial districts cannot be deliberately designed, but when the process has begun, the growth of the district can be facilitated by governmental support.

SUMMARY

This chapter completed the discussion of theories, models, and issues of internationalization that have dominated the existing literature on the internationalization processes of firms. It revisited some of the themes discussed in previous chapters, especially the concept of relationships and the network approach to internationalization. The main message of the chapter was that companies can leverage resources through collaborative arrangements with other companies and with public institutions. The increasing popularity of the hybrid set of collaborative arrangements referred to as strategic alliances was highlighted. The next chapter discusses the relevance of all the theories, models, and issues of internationalization presented thus far to the operations of companies located in developing countries.

Chapter 6

Internationalization in Developing Countries

As noted earlier, marketing activities of firms in developing countries have hitherto received limited academic interest when compared with the vast volume of literature on marketing in general. Published studies in the area have been rather intermittent and guided by no coherent theoretical or conceptual framework, and only a small group of them have addressed issues of internationalization of firms. Despite the paucity of knowledge in the area, we deem it purposeful to discuss the available literature in this chapter to provide an overview of the context within which developing country firms make decisions and organize their international business activities. The chapter also provides some insight into the relevance of the models and theories presented in the preceding chapters to the developing country situations.

MARKETING AND DEVELOPMENT

Earlier writers on the issue of marketing in developing countries have been concerned mainly with marketing problems and opportunities in these countries (Drucker, 1958; Reed, 1965; Kaynak and Hudanah, 1987). Two broad strands of research have dominated the literature. The first group covers studies aimed at highlighting the relationship between marketing and development and providing policy guidelines on how marketing activities can be developed. The second category of studies explores the opportunities and consequences of the transfer of Western marketing skills and technology to the developing countries. The first group of researchers has seen marketing as performing both adaptive and formative roles in a country's development process (Varadarajan, 1984; Kaynak and Hudanah, 1987; Kinsey, 1988). That is, marketing activities respond progressively with the development of an economy, while stimulating and reinforcing the ongoing change process in the economy. Effective marketing systems allow swift flow of goods and services to producers and consumers and therefore provide additional stimulus to the dynamic forces in an economic development process. The contemporary literature has also highlighted the roles that export marketing and export sector development can play in the development of economies (Leonidou and Katsikeas, 1996). At the macroeconomic level, exporting contributes to foreign exchange reserves of nations, provides employment, and foments forward and backward linkages within an economy. At the microlevel, export marketing provides firms with new market opportunities, thereby raising their capacity utilization and improving their financial and overall competitive positions.

Researchers, however, have noted a general lack of appreciation of marketing's dynamic role among policymakers in these countries. Marketing intermediaries are viewed by public officers with suspicion and as standing between consumers and the producers, draining the economic system of vitality. Government policies therefore tend to be rigidly regulatory and prohibitive rather than facilitatory. This offers no inducement for the private sector to undertake investments in marketing facilities or the acquisition of marketing knowledge that can improve the coordination of activities within the system. As a result, the marketing systems in most developing countries have not changed much in several decades. Expansions to existing systems, where they occur, have taken the form of additions to the old structures and not qualitative change. The potential dynamic role of marketing in the economic development process is therefore seriously constrained in most developing countries.

Based on these observations, the transfer of Western marketing technology to developing countries has been considered by some researchers as imperative for the development of these economies. The leading argument has been that the marketing systems in the developing countries must be modernized in order to serve the growing number of consumers in these countries (Mittendorf, 1982). The available evidence on modernization of channel systems and other marketing technology transfer initiatives, however, have not fully supported the optimism that some writers have expressed on the modernization of domestic marketing systems. Reusse (1976), for example, recounts several cases in which large-scale commercial storage and processing facilities remained idle in developing countries many years after their construction or were used at under 20 percent capacity simply because the domestic supply was far lower than the capacity of the new facilities. Therefore, it has been argued that, for some time to come, the marketing task in many developing countries will be to stimulate the creation of surplus rather than its disposal.

The perennial shortages of goods and services in the developing countries have serious implications for internationalization, in general, and export marketing, in particular. Such shortages underlie the attitudes and behaviors of producers and consumers in these countries and shape the experience and foundations of marketing knowledge on which managers base their export decisions and activities. It has become accepted business behavior in these countries for suppliers to deliver goods in lesser quantities and of poorer qualities than have been contracted for and to ignore delivery schedules and handle the goods with less care, without being penalized by their buyers, since alternative sources of supply are limited (Fafchamps, 1996). Producers also tend to attach less importance to workmanship, style, and packaging as product attributes. If the products perform their utilitarian functions, their appearance may, at best, be a secondary consideration (Vernon-Wortzel, Wortzel, and Deng, 1988). The high bargaining power of suppliers/producers over their customers is transmitted throughout the channel systems, leaving the final consumers without realistic options.

Under such domestic marketing conditions, producers have limited incentives to improve their marketing activities to a level required to operate competitively in a global market. They are unable to fully comprehend the implications of importers' purchase cycles, planning and budgeting, and inventory management strategies. As such, their export decisions are not likely to take due cognizance of the importers' logistics considerations. This creates problems in the supply chain management and renders their offers less competitive than offers that are based on a solid understanding of importers' performance requirements. In situations in which overseas customers have no other option than to buy from developing country producers, as importers, they painstakingly select exporters and train them to a level that would enable the exporters to schedule their production and deliveries to meet the overseas customers' requirements. In today's international competitive environment, such patient overseas customers are very rare, and "importer-pull" (buyer-driven) exports are no longer a realistic option for many firms in the developing countries (Vernon-Wortzel, Wortzel, and Deng, 1988).

It is against this background of inadequate supply and weak marketing facilities as well as poor customer-oriented domestic marketing practices that we now examine the applicability of the theories and models of internationalization to developing country firms.

APPLICABILITY OF INTERNATIONALIZATION THEORIES AND MODELS TO DEVELOPING COUNTRIES

As discussed in Chapter 1, internationalization theories and models can be grouped into three categories: (1) the Stages Models, (2) the Contingency Models, and (3) the (Inter)Action Models. This categorization has been adopted in this section's discussions.

Stages Models

To recapitulate, it is generally held in the Stages Models that the internationalization of companies takes place in a gradual and orderly manner based on learning and accumulation of experience. The initiation of export activities is believed to be preceded by domestic market expansion (Welch and Wiedersheim-Paul, 1980; Cavusgil, 1982; Leonidou and Katsikeas, 1996). This domestic market expansion offers the firms useful experience for later export activity. The literature, however, is silent on how firms develop resources and enhance their competitive capabilities in order to undertake such an expansion. Issues such as local and international sourcing arrangements, new product development, and possible diversification into other lines of business, all of which form part of the overall corporate strategy of companies are ignored in the literature (Leonidou and Katsikeas, 1996). These omissions constitute one of the major limitations of these models in analyzing the internationalization process of firms in the developing countries. As Das (1994) argues, due to severe constraints on the export performance of nascent exporters from the developing countries, these firms may have to manage a diversified portfolio of business activities to attain their overall corporate objectives. Domestic market expansion for existing products may therefore be only one of these several business activities. Furthermore, as indicated earlier, the economic situation in most developing countries does not induce proactive domestic market expansion and acquisition of marketing skills that can be subsequently transferred into export marketing activities.

The Stages Models also assume a sequential irreversible growth process of internationalization. The assumption of irreversibility appears hardly tenable in developing countries due to the sizes, ownership structures, and internationalization motives of these firms. As Vernon-Wortzel, Wortzel, and Deng (1988) argue, some firms may feel content with reaching the third stage in the internationalization process, i.e., active export involvement. They may hold no ambitions for further growth, since this may push them far beyond their optimal capacities. Studies of the internationalization of developed country firms have also shown that firms may reverse or stall in their internationalization processes (Turnbull, 1987).

Based, as they are, on learning and the gradual accumulation of experience, the Stages Models may, however, be of relevance in explaining certain aspects of the export behavior of companies in the developing countries. As argued in Chapter 2, knowledge is critical to companies' decisions to commit resources to an internationalization process (Johanson and Vahlne, 1977) Market knowledge is usually divided into objective knowledge and experiential knowledge (Eriksson et al., 1997). Little use is made of objective knowledge obtained through conventional marketing research in the internationalization processes of companies in the developed countries. It is therefore fair to assume that the developing country companies will not make any significant use of it either. Following the Stages Models, the developing country companies are most likely to acquire their market knowledge incrementally through actions and reflections on their transactional experience. The manner in which the experience is acquired will, however, depend on the nature of the export market. Some developing country companies may target their exports at the developed market economies of North America and Western Europe. Others may target culturally similar nearby markets, granting that their products enjoy competitive advantages there. Market knowledge acquisition in nearby markets may follow the expectations found in the Stages Models if the companies export the products directly and monitor the marketing process. But, where indirect market entry strategies are employed, the experience they gain may be limited. The degree of market knowledge acquired in the more distant markets of Europe and America will depend on the nature of their relationships with the overseas importers and distributors.

In sum, although most developing country companies will not preface their internationalization process with domestic market involvement, as suggested in the Stages Models, the models' assumption of gradual experiential learning about overseas markets does apply to many of the companies in the developing countries.

Contingency Models

In contrast to the Stages Models, the proponents of the Contingency Models endorse the view that the appropriateness of the internationalization strategy of a company is context specific. They therefore advise a company to identify and analyze the critical factors of the environment and the company itself before adopting a strategy. The models normally present a general checklist of conditions and the types of strategies inspired by such conditions.

The Transaction Costs Theory was presented earlier as one of the key theories within the contingency category. Following the Transaction Costs Theory, firms choose the least-cost option in deciding whether to externalize or internalize their transactions. Costs usually considered by the companies include prepurchase costs (search, evaluation, and negotiations); cost of coordination and procurement of inputs; monitoring, control, and inspection of product quality;

and the exchange process in general, as well as postpurchase costs (for example, servicing, repairs, and maintenance).

The relevance of the Transaction Costs Theory to an understanding of the internationalization processes of developing country companies can be discussed from two viewpoints. The first is its explanation of the logic likely to guide companies' internationalization decisions. The second is how overseas customers are likely to relate to developing country companies, if their decisions are guided by the assumptions underlying the Transaction Costs Theory. From the first perspective, it can be assumed that neophyte exporters from the developing countries will be highly uncertain about the outcomes of their export decisions. They may therefore seek to reduce their uncertainties by undertaking market studies. But due to their "bounded rationality," the usefulness of such market studies is likely to be limited. Thus, alternative approaches may be considered. As noted earlier, since their transactions with overseas buyers are expected to occur frequently, they may gain their market knowledge through such interactions. The importance of their relationships with foreign customers is further augmented by the necessity of making asset-specific investments (for example, facilities required for exporting fresh vegetables and fruits), as these facilities are lacking in most developing countries. Thus, collaborative arrangements with overseas customers may characterize the internationalization of developing country companies.

Turning to the expected behavior of the foreign customers toward their developing country suppliers, it can be argued that customers are likely to base their decisions on high uncertainties surrounding their transactions. The relationships may therefore entail high monitoring costs. Unless the additional monitoring costs are more than compensated for by lower prices for the goods and services exchanged, the potential foreign buyers may opt to internalize their transactions. That is, they are likely to resort to the use of hierarchies rather than depend on the markets (Buckley, 1990). If they choose to acquire their supplies from the developing country companies, some may exhibit opportunistic behavior by capitalizing on their market knowledge advantages and the inability of their developing country suppliers to monitor the transactions closely. This may hold particularly true for the smaller overseas importers, which are likely to be less worried about their reputations in the market.

Limited empirical studies have lent credence to these observations. In a study of Kenyan horticultural exports, Jaffee (1993) reported that a significant proportion of the exports is governed by intrafirm trade or long-term contractual arrangements. Thus, the importing European firms play important management and technical roles in the Kenyan firms in order to reduce uncertainties that could characterize the transactions. Decisions regarding product lines, sales volumes, delivery times, and market destinations were all done by the European partner companies. Harris-Pascal, Humphrey, and Dolan (1998) have also made similar observations in their study of supply chain management within the U.K. horticultural trade.

(Inter)Action Models

One criticism of the Transaction Costs Theory is that it ignores the view that transactions are socially embedded. That is, social norms and trust can play a significant role in reducing the need for monitoring and surveillance in market structures. This weakness has been addressed to a substantial degree in the (Inter)Action Models, in which companies are perceived as members of networks and their economic activities as being socially embedded. Internationalization means extending networks to encompass companies abroad. To do so, companies use their existing network members as a springboard to enter into overseas business networks. Internationalization in a network sense is neither a rigidly planned process nor a coincidental one. The company's position in the present network enhances its accessibility to information and opportunities.

It is therefore most likely that developing country companies will be guided predominately by social and business network relations in their internationalization strategy formulation. Different mechanisms and social bonding characterize the trust-building processes found in different countries. It has been argued that in some African countries, for example, ascribed status, familism, and ethnic links are stronger bases of trust than nonkin relations (Kuada, 1994; Sørensen and Kuada, 1997). In some Asian societies, nonkin relations constitute strong foundations for business-related trust (Hamilton and Biggart, 1988; Whitley, 1992). In Anglo-Saxon countries and continental

Europe, businesspeople tend to place their trust in rules and regulations that constitute the bedrock of the business systems.

These observations imply that the explanatory capacity of (Inter)Action Models depends on the business systems within which the target customers of developing country firms are located. As "latecomers" on the European and North American markets, manufacturing companies from developing countries may rely on companies with which they already have business relationships (e.g., as suppliers of equipment or raw materials) in order to enter the markets. Business leads from friends and relatives may also be used to a limited extent. The more proactive firms may seek information about prospective overseas buyers from export and import promotion offices established for such purposes.

As in the Stages Models, the (Inter)Action Models also consider overseas market knowledge acquisition to be critical to the internationalization processes of companies. The difference between the two sets of models lies in the market knowledge acquisition approaches to which they subscribe. The (Inter)Action Models place emphasis on network members as sources of information and the basis for knowledge generation. The more centrally positioned a company is within a network, the greater its accessibility to market knowledge. In contrast, experience acquired through independent actions may form the primary basis of market knowledge in the Stages Models.

KEY ISSUES OF INTERNATIONALIZATION FROM A DEVELOPING COUNTRY PERSPECTIVE

The discussions in Chapters 2 through 5 have highlighted the following as being among the main issues featured in the literature on export marketing:

- International market knowledge acquisition methods and process
- Motives of internationalization and selection of foreign markets
- Choice of foreign market entry strategies
- Interfirm relations and links between the public and business sectors of economies

This section discusses the relevance of the views on these issues as expressed in the literature to the internationalization process of developing country firms.

International Market Knowledge Acquisition in Developing Countries

The discussions in Chapter 2 show that firms embarking on export activities can acquire foreign market knowledge from four main sources: (1) action and experience, (2) information acquired by using conventional market research methods, (3) transfers from people possessing the required knowledge or consultants, and (4) dialogues with members of their networks. Although these sources of knowledge are not necessarily mutually exclusive, managers' relative preference for them will depend on their management orientation and personality. A manager with a planning orientation will normally show a strong preference for information acquired through the use of conventional market research techniques, the action-oriented manager will show a stronger preference for an experiential approach to market knowledge acquisition, while the network-oriented manager will consider information acquired through dialogues as more reliable. It has also been indicated that even firms having a strong preference for the use of market research methods differ in terms of the degree of sophistication of the techniques used (Lim, Sharkey, and Kim, 1996). Firms with higher degrees of export involvement tend to use more sophisticated techniques, whereas those at the initial stages of their export involvement adopt simple data collection techniques, such as consultations with business associates combined with intuitive evaluations of their overseas market opportunities (Calof, 1993).

Developing country firms should not differ substantially from developed country firms with regard to their approaches to market knowledge acquisition. This chapter's review of internationalization has shown that most developing country firms will exhibit a stronger preference for experiential approaches to market knowledge acquisition for four main reasons: First, most of them are relatively small entrepreneurial firms at their initial stages of internationalization, with limited resources for undertaking conventional market research even if they consider such an approach to be intellectually appealing. Second, the volume of their exports is relatively low, and as such, sales to even a single overseas distributor will be sufficient for them to attain their export goals. Third, some of the manufacturing firms may initiate the internationalization process through contract production for European and/or North American firms and, therefore, may not require independent market analysis for an initial entry into the market. Fourth, to the extent that the internationalization strategies of firms depend on their network positions, they will find information from network members to be most reliable.

Motives of Internationalization and Market Selection of Companies in Developing Countries

As noted earlier, the contention that most companies must have strong domestic market bases before venturing abroad runs counter to the operational conditions found in most developing countries. First, the small sizes of the home markets of firms in most developing countries do not offer them opportunities to enjoy economies of scale and growth through the accumulation and use of domestic resources. Second, the noncompetitive nature of the home markets for certain products does not offer developing country firms the challenges necessary to develop product characteristics suitable for the highly competitive markets of the Triad economies. Third, the sluggishness of economic growth in most of the developing countries makes it difficult for firms to acquire their first export experience from relatively similar market environments—i.e., from nearby markets. In situations in which the degree of competition within the domestic market increases due to trade liberalization, the local enterprises may be severely disadvantaged by their relatively lower marketing experience and weaker resource bases.

Even for products having huge domestic markets, it is not at all certain that the size and dynamics of the domestic market will provide the firms with the necessary training, resources, and motivation to go abroad. A viable domestic market may actually discourage firms from making efforts to expand internationally. By restricting their market perceptions to their domestic environments, the firms may become ethnocentric in their strategic dispositions and avoid raising the levels of their production beyond domestic market demands.

But even where the motivation exists to go abroad at an early point in their history, firms in the developing countries are likely to be faced with other handicaps; for example, most of their managers may lack the required skills and time for studying the often confusing foreign business regulations and procedures that characterize business relations with customers in other countries. In other words, the managerial characteristics that motivate exporting should be assumed to be basically lacking. Export motives can therefore be only external and reactive. Internal motives, to the extent that they exist at all, are likely to be opportunistic, based on the belief that the rewards of exporting will offset the problems and difficulties involved.

These observations raise a fundamental question about the underlying motives and processes of internationalization of firms in the developing countries. Obviously, to the extent that firms internationalize their operations in the developing countries (and an increasing number of firms are involved in export), the dominant internationalization motives and processes of these firms may differ from those reported in the existing literature.

Arguably, business owners are usually relatively few and geographically concentrated, providing them with the opportunity to create various collaborative frameworks to support their operations. The collective orientation of an industry toward exports may also be a consequence of (or reinforced by) the benefits of resource sharing that could be derived from various forms of collaboration among firms. If firms in a given industry embrace exports as a viable growth strategy, they are likely to develop horizontal and vertical relationships that support such a strategy. Internationalization then becomes an entire industry or sector strategy rather than business strategies pursued by isolated firms. Such a collective orientation will increase the quality and amount of export-related information that circulates within the industry.

Market choice of these firms will be influenced by a variety of factors. Prominent among them are: (1) established industry traditions, (2) available marketing information, (3) government trade link arrangements, and (4) the nature of products exported. New exporters within an industry may be influenced by the "demonstration effect" of decisions made by industry members with more export experience. That is, they simply look for distributors in countries where other firms sell their products. Those firms who initiate their internationalization through contract production for outsourcing firms based in the developed countries do not engage in independent market selection decisions.

Choice of Market Entry and Development Mode

Choice of market entry mode for developing country firms will again depend on their motives for embarking on the internationalization process, the nature of their products, the resources at their disposal, as well as the markets for which the products are earmarked. Firms producing technologically innovative products may opt for direct export or licensing. Since they are likely to have limited resources at their disposal, the probability that they will opt for equity joint ventures or green field investments is quite low during the initial stages of internationalization. Other firms are likely to choose direct or indirect modes of entry, again depending on their levels of involvement and commitment in the internationalization process. Thus, it is reasonable to assume that most developing country firms face a very limited range of choices for entry modes.

Few writers have examined the internationalization process of firms from an input perspective (Welch and Luostarinen, 1993). Internationalization is seen here as the extent to which firms are linked with overseas suppliers to acquire their raw materials, inputs, and technology. In this regard, developing country firms may initiate their internationalization process, by identifying and interacting with vendors abroad, either on an arms-length basis or on a longstanding contractual basis. Such linkages may also offer them the opportunity to gain access to relevant business networks abroad for subsequent export strategy development. This perspective to the internationalization process of firms in the developing countries is discussed in greater detail in Chapter 12.

Relationships Between Public Institutions and Business in Developing Countries

The discussion of (Inter)Action Models indicated that internationalization of firms may be greatly facilitated by network relations, interfirm collaborative arrangements such as strategic alliances, and continuous government-business dialogues based on partnership and mutual interest. In network terms, exporters from developing countries can be characterized as "late starters" and may therefore face many difficulties in their internationalization processes. In particular, it is very likely that the inexperienced among them will run into importers and agents abroad with opportunistic inclinations, simply because they do not have the resources to attract foreign partners who seek stable and large-scale supply relationships based on trust and long-term cooperation.

The relevance of strategic alliances to the internationalization process of developing country firms should be viewed in terms of the transfer of improved quality inputs as well as technical and managerial know-how from firms based in the developed market economies to those in the developing countries. The collaborations may be arranged to cover most of the value-added activities of the developing country company, or they may focus on just a few key activities, e.g., production or marketing. Thus, through an international strategic alliance, Ghanaian firms can consolidate their production and marketing activities on the domestic market and gradually acquire a base upon which a competitive export advantage can be developed. Thus, strategic alliances are not a direct internationalization instrument for Ghanaian firms. Production contracts, however, deserve special mention. Production contracts are strategic alliances whereby local enterprises produce according to the design and methods of foreign producers. Production contracts are especially prevalent in the textile, clothing, and shoe industries. For some reason, foreign contract production is little known in Ghana, apparently because Ghana, and Africa in general, is outside the sourcing race by MNCs for gaining competitive advantage. A key question for firms in countries such as Ghana is, What contributions can they make to their developed country partner firms in a strategic alliance in return for technical and managerial upgrading?

With regard to government-business relations, it can be noted that analysts of business systems acknowledge the importance of the state's role in the management of economic activities (Whitley, 1992; Whitley, 1994). Thus, the policy formulation process of the state machinery (conventionally understood as political process) is important to an understanding of business systems development. It has been established that the state is heavily involved in business sector development in most Asian economies (Hamilton and Biggart, 1988; Whitley, 1990). In other regions of the developing world, such as Latin America and Africa, governments have been advised by multilateral aid organizations such as the World Bank to decrease their direct involvement in business due to the poor performance of state-owned enterprises (SOEs), in particular, and parastatal businesses, in general. However, considering the low level of development of facilities that can reduce transactional costs and enhance business sector development in these regions of the world, the authors have argued that a dynamic interaction between the state institutions and the business sector in most developing countries is imperative for their development (see also Sørensen, 1994b). The establishment of mechanisms that encourage continuous dialogue will reduce misunderstandings and suspicions between the state institutions and business organizations, thereby forming the basis for trust, commitment, and joint actions to promote economic growth at both macro- and microlevels.

In summary, relationships through networks and strategic alliances may promote upstream and downstream forms of internationalization in developing economies such as Ghana. To succeed, government institutions' relations with the business community must be based on dialogue rather than patron-client arrangements. The discussion of the empirical investigations in Part II of this book will endeavor to explore the extent to which relationships influence the internationalization process in Ghana today, as well as efforts currently undertaken to strengthen both interfirm and government-business relationships.

SUMMARY

The gradual, experiential market knowledge acquisition process described in the Stages Models has relevance for an analysis of the internationalization process of developing country companies. However, the models' description of market choice decision may not fully apply. Possibilities of developing country companies targeting geographically distant and culturally dissimilar markets may be expected.

Suggestions contained in the Contigency Models that internationalization strategies are context specific have a general relevance for developing country companies as well. Although the conditions for internalization suggested in the Transaction Costs Theory may not apply entirely, some degree of collaborative arrangement between developing and developed country companies can be expected to take place as a means of reducing transactional uncertainties that may surround their business relations.

The (Inter)Action Models, in general, and the Network Theory, in particular, hold promising analytical insights for the internationalization process of developing country companies. Again, the increasing importance of hybrid collaborative arrangements between firms the world over suggests that developing country companies can leverage resources from local and overseas companies to upgrade their technological and managerial capabilities.

PART II:
EMPIRICAL EVIDENCE

The preceding six chapters provided the reader with an overview of the leading theories/models and issues that have received increased attention in the academic literature on the internationalization of firms. It was repeatedly stressed in the discussions that these theories, models, and issues have been adopted by mature market economies as their frame of reference. However, attempts were made in Chapter 6 to examine their relevance to the study of the internationalization process of firms in developing countries, such as Ghana.

Part II explores empirically the applicability of the theories in the Ghanaian context. Chapter 7 presents the profile of Ghana and the political as well as economic context within which exporters operate. Chapters 8 through 11 discuss the results of the empirical investigation, examining the main characteristics of the exporting firms and analyzing their export motives and how they acquire market knowledge, select markets, and choose entry strategies. The perceptions and interactions between government institutions and firms are taken up in Chapter 11.

Empirical research on the internationalization of Ghanaian companies is scanty. The most recent and comprehensive study was conducted by Baah-Nuakoh and colleagues (1996). They interviewed 150 companies, including 40 exporters from the traditional and nontraditional sectors to assess the impact of the structural adjustment programs on the Ghanaian economy. Whereas the study by Baah-Nuakoh and others dwells on macroeconomic issues, the present study focuses on the microeconomic or management issues of internationalization.

We caution the reader that the empirical investigation reported here is based on only twenty firms producing/exporting nontraditional products, allowing for only limited generalizability of the conclusions drawn. However, as an exploratory study, the evidence provides some useful insights.

Chapter 7

Ghana: Country Profile and Setting for the Empirical Study

Ghana is a West African country located in the middle of the Guinea Coast. It is bordered to the east by Togo and to the west by Côte d'Ivoire (Ivory Coast). It also shares a borders with Burkina Faso to the north, while the Gulf of Guinea forms its southern border. Ghana's location provides the country with comparative advantages over its neighboring Sahel countries in the production of tropical food products such as cereals, root crops, fruits and vegetables, as well as in the processing of salt. Other things being equal, there must be good market opportunities for these products in the nearby countries.

The country became a British colony in 1845 after three centuries of active trading with European merchants. Ghana gained political independence from Britain in March 1957. In general terms, political authority in Ghana has been consistently centralized, both before and during the aftermath of political independence. It has either taken the form of a one-party civilian monopoly, as under Kwame Nkrumah (1957-1966), or a military dictatorship. This fact bears on the formulation and implementation of major economic policies that form the context of business development in the country. First, democratic decision-making processes at top political levels have been lacking. Since policies of military regimes did not require the endorsement of the citizens and the governments were not held accountable for their decisions, there has been no pressure on them to undertake continual judicious assessment of their decisions. Second, the administrative class of the country (i.e., the civil servants) and the military rulers did not share a common educational background and career aspirations. Therefore, no firm basis existed for the administrative and political institutions to evolve a common and committed approach to development in the country. Third, each successive military government saw its period of administration as temporary, i.e., to prepare the way for a new civilian administration. Thus, apart from Rawlings's second military government (1982-1992), none of the military governments considered long-term coherent economic development a primary objective.

On the macroeconomic front, successive governments have shown remarkable mistrust of private capitalism and the market system. Under the Nkrumah government, ideologically, the state was considered the most legitimate custodian of national wealth and a guarantor of the collective social benefits of the people. Other governments during the 1960s and 1970s (with the exception of the Busia government, 1969-1972) showed similar distrust of markets as effective and fair resource-allocating mechanisms (Huq, 1989). The allocation of economic resources through administrative mechanisms, however, has been fraught with serious weaknesses.

Similar to many other African countries, Ghana experienced two decades of serious economic hardships between 1965 and 1985, largely due to unsuccessful experiments with state entrepreneurship, discouragement of private capital accumulation, and poor management and undisciplined implementation of economic policies (Huq, 1989; Nugent, 1995). The immediate decline that occurred in all major sectors of the economy was combined with high rates of inflation (reaching 120 percent annually in the early 1980s) as well as a destabilization of the state budget. At the same time, the population was growing at an annual rate of 3 percent, with urban population growth at about 5 percent, leading to severe pressure on supplies of all goods and services and a high rate of unemployment, particularly in urban areas (see Loxley, 1988, for a detailed account).

Starting in 1984, the Rawlings government initiated a series of economic policies under the World Bank-sponsored structural adjustment program (SAP) aimed at a reversal of Ghana's economic decline. The key elements of the economic recovery program included liberalization of prices, rationalization and privatization of SOEs, exitensive infrastructural rehabilitation projects, and legal provisions aimed at improvement of the overall investment climate in the country.[1] Public-sector employees were redeployed in large numbers, while fees were introduced in education, health, and other social sectors.

EXPORT SECTOR DEVELOPMENT POLICY IN GHANA

Export sector development, as part of a general liberalization of the trade and investment regime, has assumed a central position in Ghana's economic policy since the introduction of the SAP. Key objectives in the current export strategies are as follows:

1. The diversification of the export base of the economy, i.e., a move away from dependence on a few primary export commodities by means of encouraging the exportation of a wider range of products classified as "nontraditional" exports[2]
2. Increasing the volume and/or value of the various export products
3. Increasing the number of firms engaged in export business

Government export promotional schemes since 1991 include the following:

1. The provision of income tax rebates based on the proportion of outputs exported by the manufacturing firms in a given year
2. One hundred percent retention of export earnings made by exporters of nontraditional exports for purposes of financing the importation of inputs
3. Customs duty drawback scheme under which exporters can reclaim all import duties paid on inputs used in the production of export products

Recent figures show, however, that Ghana's export sector remains undiversified. The contribution of nontraditional exports to total export earnings continues to be modest, between 6.7 and 22 percent.[3] Furthermore, although the number of nontraditional export products has increased in recent years, from 164 in 1992 to 270 in 1997, earnings from these export items, however, amounted only to US$329 million in 1997, up from US$68.4 million in 1992 and US$276.2 million in 1996. The number of exporters of nontraditional products has varied over the years, from 3,188 in 1992, down to 1,980 in 1993, and up again in 1995 to 2,802 exporters and in 1997 to 3,278 (Institute of Statistical, Social, and Economic Research [ISSER], 1998). Apart from the increase in the number of firms and the products exported, the direction of export trade has also changed to some extent. The share of the top ranking four countries—Germany, the United Kingdom, the United States, and the Netherlands—has dropped from 63 percent in 1990, to 46.9 percent in 1992, up a bit to 50.3 percent in 1993, and down again to 41.7 percent in 1995, implying a widening of the export market base.

The continuous export concentration on raw materials and primary commodities makes Ghana's export earnings very dependent on the precarious world commodity market. In this market, there is little room for competitive strategy initiatives compared to exports from manufacturing industries. Getting many Ghanaian firms to become active players in the international business arena is, therefore, a pressing national goal.

KEY ECONOMIC SECTORS

Two main sectors make direct significant contributions to Ghana's nontraditional export business development: are the agricultural and industrial sectors. The growth of the agricultural sector (which accounted for 39.2 percent of the gross domestic product [GDP] in 1997) has been erratic since 1984, with some years showing negative growth. The average growth in 1985 to 1989 was 2.3 percent and 1.1 percent between 1990 and 1994 (ISSER, 1998, p. 89). In 1995, this sector recorded a substantial growth of 4.2 percent, mainly as a result of favorable climatic conditions. However, it has since then experienced steady decline, to 4 percent in 1996 and 3.3 percent in 1997, barely above the population growth rate of 3.1 percent that year.[4] Consistent with the general decline in agricultural production, growth within the food subsector has also declined. The available empirical evidence shows a significant decline in the yields and areas under cultivation for most of the major crops (ISSER, 1998).

Since most of the country's nontraditional exports come from the agricultural sector, the downward trend in production must be expected to have adverse impact on the growth within that export subsector, particularly by constraining the exporters' ability to meet delivery commitments at profit. Between 1996 and 1997, the volume of exports of major nontraditional agricultural products, such as pineapple, kola nut, and vegetables, declined by between 9 and 30 percent. However, the volume of exports of other products such as cashew nuts, mangoes, avocados, bananas, and watermelons increased during the same period, largely because there is a limited domestic market for them. Thus, although the overall performance of the nontraditional agricultural exports improved (partly due to the increase in the number of items exported), the decline in the volumes of exports of the major items reflects a weak supply response to the export sector development efforts of the government.

The industrial sector in Ghana includes manufacturing, mining and quarrying, electricity, water, and construction. The overall industry growth rate has been unstable as well. The figures between 1984 and 1997 show a growth rate ranging from 11.9 percent in 1984 to 1.3 percent in 1994. The average growth rate between 1984 and 1988 was 11.2 percent while the average growth rate between 1989 to 1997 was barely 4.2 percent. The growth rate during recent three successive years (1995-1997), however, has shown an upward trend. After the lowest growth rate of 1.3 percent in 1994, industry growth increased to 3.3 percent in 1995, 4.2 percent in 1996, and 5.7 percent in 1997 (ISSER, 1998).[5] However, the rate dropped sharply to 2.5 percent in 1998, mainly due to a severe energy crisis in the country during the greater part of 1997 and into 1998.

The manufacturing sector is the major contributor to the export sector within the broader industrial sector. Growth within the manufacturing sector has also shown an upward trend in recent years, rising from 1.5 percent in 1994 to 1.8 percent in 1995, and increasing further to 3 percent in 1996 and 5.4 percent in 1997. The manufacturing sector's share of GDP has accordingly moved upward, from 7.2 percent in 1984 to 9.1 percent in 1997.

The recent positive growth trends within the industrial sector, in general, and the manufacturing sector, in particular, have been attributed to the effects of two government policies. First, the privatization of over sixty state-owned enterprises between 1995 and 1997 has brought the total number of privatized firms to 201. The new owners

have invested substantially to upgrade the technology and managerial capacities of the firms to improve their operational efficiencies.
Second, the establishment of an export free zone in Ghana in 1995
has attracted some additional investments within the manufacturing
sector. Out of the thirty-seven enterprises approved to operate in the
export-processing zones at the end of 1997, twenty-six of them were
manufacturing firms (ISSER, 1998). The effects of these developments are now reflected in the increasing contribution of the
manufacturing sector to the overall performance of Ghana's nontraditional export sector. About 82 percent of the nontraditional exports in 1997 were classified as processed or semiprocessed; cocoa
butter, canned tuna, and sliced veneer now count among the major
nontraditional exports.

Other subsectors within the industrial sector have fared rather
poorly in recent years. Electricity and water supplies have been the
poorest performing industries. Since the country is heavily dependent on hydroelectrical power supply, changes in the water level of
the Akosombo Dam create havoc for the entire economy. It has
been suggested that the manufacturing sector might have performed
better than the previous figures had it not been for the electricity
crisis in 1997 and 1998, caused mainly by the fall in the water level
in the dam.

RESEARCH DESIGN AND DATA COLLECTION

Data for the empirical part of the study were collected from the top
twenty exporters of nontraditional export products in Ghana in 1995.
The sampling frame was a list of exporting companies registered with
the Ghana Export Promotion Council (GEPC). This register constitutes
the most reliable sampling frame because nearly all exporters are
registered with the council. Twenty-five leading exporting firms (i.e.,
those with export sales of more than US$100,000 per year) from three
product categories were initially contacted by mail to participate in the
study. This was followed up by telephone calls and personal visits to
ascertain their reaction to our requests and also to screen their appropriateness for the purposes of the study. Out of the twenty-five
firms contacted, twenty of them agreed to participate in the study and,
therefore, constitute the final sample. All the firms are located in

Accra, the capital of Ghana, even though location was not a specific criterion for selection. Some of them, however, have their production units outside Accra. In light of the exploratory nature of the present study, we do not consider the small sample to be a handicap to the analysis of and conclusions from the data. The main value of the results lies in the issues raised and the direction the results give for further research into the export sector development process.

The research technique adopted was a structured personal interview with owner-managers of the twenty firms. Limiting the list of respondents to owner-managers helps reduce the incidence of "source-of-measurement errors" caused by respondents' ignorance of specific facts of their operations. The interviews were conducted with the assistance of two MBA (master of business administration) students of the School of Administration, University of Ghana, who were employed as research assistants for the project. The local knowledge of the two students was invaluable in establishing contacts with the firms and their managers and in establishing rapport with them during the interviews.

The interviewing process itself was facilitated by an especially positive attitude of all the respondents toward the study. The interviews lasted between two and three hours, with a minimum of two interviewers in attendance. Most of the respondents scheduled the interviews after normal working hours or during the less busy periods of the day (or even on Saturdays) to avoid excessive interruptions. These conditions enabled us to gain more penetrating insights into their operations than would otherwise have been possible. The interviews therefore represent a valid assessment of the experience upon which Ghanaian exporters base their decisions and actions.

For all the interviews, data reduction began with detailed interview write-ups soon after the interviews were completed. These write-ups summarized the interviews in a consistent manner; follow-up data were collected (where necessary) to address problems of omission and clarity.

SUMMARY

During the first three decades of Ghana's economic history, government policies have been mainly characterized by mistrust of private capitalism. However, unsuccessful experiments with state entrepreneurship led to the decision of the present government to embark upon the structural adjustment program in 1984 with the support of IMF and the World Bank. The generally liberalized policies of the past fifteen years have encouraged the establishment of new private-owned export firms. In addition to this, the government has embarked upon export promotion policies aimed at broadening the export base of the economy and increasing the volume of exports. Income tax rebates, customs duty drawback schemes, and 100 percent retention of export earnings have been among the incentives provided by the government to encourage export business in the country. Some progress has been made, but the performance of the export sector remains far below the government target. The empirical results reported in the subsequent chapters provide some insight into the profile and strategies of the newly established exporting firms and factors militating against their growth.

Chapter 8

Profile of the Firms
and Their Management

The theoretical discussions in Part I drew attention to relationships between certain key characteristics of firms and their export performance potentials. For example, it was suggested that the degree of export intensity and the resource commitment of firms depend on their size. Furthermore, the degree of international exposure and the experience of key managers are believed to have a powerful influence on their export decisions. Dichtl, Koglmayr, and Mueller (1990) describe the non-foreign-market-oriented managers as having the following characteristics:

- See foreign countries/markets as very dissimilar to their own countries/domestic markets
- Are old and have limited education
- Are less proficient in foreign languages
- Are risk averse, rigid, and unwilling to change
- Display a principally negative attitude toward exporting as a possible company strategy

Firms whose key decision makers fit these characteristics are not expected to enter export business or to take such activities seriously.

These observations make it worthwhile to begin the empirical discussions with a profile of the firms that participated in the study. The central question addressed in this chapter is whether firms covered in this study have the required characteristics to become giant players in their respective lines of business at the international level. We approach this question by taking a look at the background and history of the firms, the products they deal in, their size, as well as their ownership structures and management. With respect to management, we consider factors such as educational background and previous work experience of the founders of the firms, their motives for entering business, as well as their degree of international business exposure. Due to sample size limitations, no statistical analysis has been made to determine the degree of association between these variables and export performance of the firms. Some of the evidence, however, is presented in tables for analytical convenience.

BACKGROUND AND OPERATIONAL HISTORY OF THE FIRMS

Most of the firms covered in this study are of recent origin. As shown in Table 8.1, 50 percent of the firms were established between 1980 and 1990. In fact, as many as 25 percent were formed after 1985, i.e., they were barely ten years old at the time of data collection. Only 15 percent of the firms were established before 1970, and 35 percent were established between 1970 and 1980. This corroborates a similar study by Baah-Nuakoh and colleagues (1996), in which the leading exporting firms were found to be relatively young (i.e., established later than firms with minor export activity). The ages of the firms in their sample were between fourteen and twenty-six years.

TABLE 8.1. Year of Establishment/Categories of Firms

Year	Non-processed food items		Processed food items		Nonfood raw materials		Light manufac-tures		Total	
	No.	%	No.	%	No.	%	No.	%	No.	%
Before 1970	1	5	1	5	—	—	1	5	3	15
1970-1980	3	15	—	—	1	5	3	15	7	35
1980-1990	5	25	1	5	1	5	3	15	10	50
Total	9	45	2	10	2	10	7	35	20	100

The short operational history of these exporting firms contrasts sharply with evidence from empirical investigations conducted in Western industrialized countries, where firms, particularly those in the larger countries, have a relatively long domestic operational history before venturing abroad. It is worth noting, however, that none of the firms surveyed were established after 1990.

A breakdown of the data shows that exporters of nonprocessed food items are of more recent origin than exporters of processed food items and manufactured items. Apparently, whereas firms with products in the latter categories were established initially to cater for domestic demand, those with products in the former category were established with the aim of serving foreign customers.

Some evidence of the firms' history of internationalization is provided in Table 8.2. For most firms, internationalization commences immediately or a few years after establishment. Twenty-five percent started exporting the same year they were established; another 25 percent started one to three years after the year of their establishment. In other words, half the firms interviewed had little or no operational experience before entering the international business arena. Most of these early starters, however, deal in nonpro-

TABLE 8.2. Year of Commencement of Export Activities/Categories of Firms

Year	Non-processed food items		Processed food items		Nonfood raw materials		Light manufac-tures		Total	
	No.	%	No.	%	No.	%	No.	%	No.	%
Same as year of es-tablishment	4	20	—	—	—	—	1	5	5	25
1 to 3 years after estab-lishment	4	20	—	—	—	—	2	10	6	30
4 to 6 years after estab-lishment	1	5	—	—	—	—	2	10	3	15
Over 6 years after estab-lishment	—	—	2	10	2	10	2	10	6	30
Total	9	45	2	10	2	10	7	35	20	100

cessed food items such as yams and fresh pineapples. Over half of the firms exporting light manufactures started exporting four or more years after the commencement of their business. This is yet another indication that they were established initially to serve the domestic market. As will be shown subsequently, entrepreneurs establish many of the firms with substantial trading experience in other areas. This evidence is supported by the investigation of Baah-Nuakoh and colleagues (1996). The manufacturing firms in that study entered the export business more than five years after their establishment.

Out of the five firms that started exporting more than six years after their establishment (see Table 8.2), two deal in processed food items (fruit juice and beer), two others deal in nonfood raw materials (cottonseed and cattle horn), and one deals in textiles. One can tentatively argue from this evidence that nonprocessed food dealers enter the export business more quickly than exporters of other nontraditional products.

On the face of it, the evidence that firms enter the export business immediately after being established runs counter to the accepted perspective in the contemporary literature which holds that firms commence exporting after many years of operation in the domestic market. (See the discussions of export motives in Chapter 3.) This inference, however, needs to be treated with some caution. A closer analysis of the data indicates that 45 percent of the firms can be classified as export trading companies, whose article of incorporation defines exporting as their primary business (see Table 8.3).

TABLE 8.3. Classification of Firms by Products

Product Categories	Production and Exporting		Exporting Only		Total	
	No.	%	No.	%	No.	%
Nonprocessed food items	3	15	6	30	9	45
Processed food items	2	10	—	—	2	10
Nonfood raw materials	—	—	2	10	2	10
Light manufactures	6	30	1	5	7	35
Total	11	55	9	45	20	100

These firms do not have any production facilities; their activities are limited to the sourcing, marketing, and distribution sides of the value chain. This holds true particularly for most of the nonprocessed food dealers, but also for dealers in handicrafts, cottonseed and cattle horn, all of whom are basically engaged in collecting, sorting, and selling the products in which they deal. (See Appendix B for a list of the firms and their product lines.)

FIRM SIZE AND PRODUCT LINES

As discussed in Part I, firm size is considered in the existing literature as a significant determinant of export motivation and performance, although the available empirical evidence is not entirely conclusive on this issue. We have, therefore, considered it purposeful to have some indication of the size of the firms covered in the present study. Since many of the respondents declined to provide us with specific data on their assets and production volume, we have used the number of full-time employees as a proxy indicator of firm size, mindful of its limitations.

In Table 8.4, we apply a classification normally used by researchers in Ghana to determine the relative sizes of local firms. The data show that 55 percent of the firms have over 100 full-time employees, while 30 percent have between five and thirty employees. Only one has fewer than five employees. Thus, although most of the firms may be classified as small by international standards, they may be considered medium-sized by Ghanaian standards, measured in terms of number of employees. The trading firms, however, are generally smaller, having fewer than thirty full-time employees and making substantial use of casual employees in connection with collecting and sorting the products they export. Firms engaged in production are relatively larger, with 100 or more full-time employees.

The relatively small sizes of the trading firms are indicative of the low entry barriers in this export subsector and the consequent vulnerability of the existing firms to tougher competition from firms with substantial resources. As will be discussed subsequently,

TABLE 8.4. Number of Full-Time Employees/Categories of Firms

Full-time employees	Non-processed food items		Processed food items		Nonfood raw materials		Light manufac-tures		Total	
	No.	%	No.	%	No.	%	No.	%	No.	%
Under 5	1	5	—	—	—	—	—	—	1	5
5-30	5	25	—	—	1	5	1	5	7	35
31-100	1	5	—	—	—	—	1	5	2	10
Over 100	2	10	2	10	1	5	5	25	10	50
Total	9	45	2	10	2	10	7	35	20	100

however, the probability of new entrants into the various product subsectors depends on the sizes and growth rates of the potential markets. Thus, a recent GEPC analysis showed only a gradual increase in the number of firms entering the agricultural export subsector, from 1,206 exporters in 1994 to 1,280 in 1995. In comparison, the number of exporters who entered the processed and semiprocessed export subsector increased from 1,154 in 1994 to 1,330 in 1995 and recorded a 67 percent increase in earnings during that period.

Table 8.3 presents a breakdown of the firms in terms of four main product categories: nonprocessed food items, processed food items, nonfood raw materials, and light manufactures. Nine of the firms deal in nonprocessed food items such as yams, pineapples, and cashew nuts. As suggested earlier, only three of these firms engage in direct production of the products that they sell; the rest operate as export trading companies. Out of the remaining eleven firms, two deal in processed food items (fruit juice and beer), two deal in nonfood raw materials (cottonseed and cattle horn), and seven deal in light manufactures.

This composition of firms and their product lines are consistent with the general trend of development within the nontraditional export sector. GEPC analysis of the sector's performance in 1995 revealed that horticultural products (pineapples, yams, and bananas) contributed 42 percent to the agricultural export subsector's earnings in that year. Fish and seafood products contributed approximately

27 percent to the earnings. A total of 1,280 exporters were registered within the agricultural subsector. This accounted for nearly 45 percent of all registered nontraditional exporters for that year. Most of them were very small, with limited export capacities.

Tremendous performance improvements have been recorded for the processed and semiprocessed subsector as well. This subsector is very broad, including all the product categories classified as processed food items and light manufactures. The GEPC figures show that 1,330 exporters exported 144 items under those categories in 1995. Pineapple juice, wood products, aluminium products, and textiles were among the key items exported that year.

OWNERSHIP STRUCTURE AND MANAGEMENT

All the firms are established as limited liability companies in accordance with Ghanaian business laws. With the exception of three, all of them are owned by family members or by a group of friends, usually with the same ethnic background. In the exclusively family-owned businesses, the male head typically holds 70 percent of the equity, the wife, 20 to 25 percent, and the children, around 10 percent. In most cases, the immediate family members actively participate in the management of the firms, although deliberate attempts are made to limit the number of extended family members employed in the firms.

Placing family members in key management positions is a characteristic feature of small private firms in Ghana, and the arguments in its support are quite persuasive. It ensures loyalty and commitment of top management to organizational decisions and tasks, since ownership is not divorced from management. However, such laudable expectations may occasionally be belied, and instruments to redress the problem of noncooperative family members may be limited. However, no such problems were alluded to in our interviews.

The restriction of ownership to family members derives from the fundamental motivations underlying the entrepreneurs' decision to enter into business. The two dominant motives may be termed (1) a survival seeking motive and (2) an opportunity/achievement motive.

Judging from the circumstances that have precipitated their decision to enter into business, it is fair to say that many of the entrepreneurs can be described as opportunity seekers. That is, they entered
business to improve their economic welfare. This holds true, for
example, for the founder of a leading fruit juice producing company
(Astek Limited), who in 1975 resigned from the Ghana Standards
Board (GSB) and opened his first quality control laboratory. Similarly, the founder of a major pineapple exporter (Combined Farmers) decided to go into farming a few years prior to his retirement,
having realized that his pension allowance could not sustain his
living standard. The present owner of Scanstyle (a furniture exporting company) bought the company from its original Norwegian
owner because it provided him with a singular opportunity to become self-employed. Other proprietors interviewed gave similar
reasons. For all these people, the decision to invest in one's own
firm was a daring one because it meant betting one's meager savings on a highly uncertain future. The fear of social and economic
deprivation in their old age, however, outweighed the anxieties of
entrepreneurship. They were all prepared to make significant initial
sacrifices and to invest the commitment necessary to succeed.

There is, however, another group of firms whose proprietors did
not face a desperate need to establish an economic base for themselves and their children. These people began with a solid economic
base. For example, the founder of a major seafood exporting company (Kiku Company Limited) had a number of businesses, including a pharmacy and a private legal practice. He decided on the
seafood business out of the sheer ambition to build a business in an
area hitherto ignored by other Ghanaian entrepreneurs. The proprietor of Getrade (handicrafts) started exporting handicrafts because
he wanted to do something on his own that was a significant benefit
for the country, having served as managing director for an international firm. These are examples of an achievement or opportunity
motive.

The two types of motives will influence the investment decisions
of the proprietors in different ways. Whereas the survival seekers
are likely to play it safe and follow growth incrementally, the opportunity seekers are apt to be more daring in the face of risks. The

implications of the two motives for export promotion schemes will be examined subsequently.

For some of these local entrepreneurs, the export business is but one of several businesses in which they are currently engaged. This diversification strategy is adopted as a means of hedging against any dramatic downturn in any of the lines of engagement as well as a possible change in government policies. This is consistent with the previously noted economic survival motive of entering into business.

DEMOGRAPHIC PROFILE OF THE PROPRIETORS AND MANAGERS

Age

All the owners are in their fifties. Many of them started their businesses in their midforties. Their age has been of significant importance to understanding the nature of their business decisions. As Lessem (1989) vividly argues, an individual manager undergoes phases of managerial development. Managers in their twenties are usually characterized by the desire for exploration, experimentation, enthusiasm, and enterprise. In their thirties, managers generally tend to emphasize consolidation, responsibility, clarity, and structure in their behavior. Reflection and self-discovery characterize midlife periods, while maturity focuses on stability.

Placing this argument within the Ghanaian sociocultural context, one should see most of the proprietors as being mature and highly aware of their family responsibilities. The combination of their age and sociocultural roles and expectations doubtlessly influences their management decisions and risk perception (Kuada, 1994).

Educational Background

About 75 percent of the firms were formed by people with higher education, i.e., university degrees. Astek's founder holds a PhD in chemistry and was a university professor before entering public service as part of the GSB. Kiku's founder has a law degree and is a practicing lawyer. The owners of Scanstyle and Combined Farmers have professional certificates in commerce and banking. Getrade is owned by the former managing director of Johnson Wax, who holds a degree in economics. This impressive academic background, combined with their previous work experience in management positions, provides the proprietors with a solid basis for understanding the operational environment of modern business as well as a set of valuable personal contacts that provide access to resources.

This background appears to have influenced their risk perception and choice of industry. For example, Kiku Company Limited is in a high-risk, relatively capital-intensive line of business where careful deliberations have to guide business decisions and the negative consequences of wrong decisions can be relatively high. Similarly, Combined Farmers started as a pioneer in commercial pineapple farming in Ghana, with no local experience on which to rely.

Comparatively, proprietors of the remaining 25 percent of the firms have modest or no formal education. Sulleyman Company— a leading exporter of kola nuts—was started by a tailor without any formal education. He, however, teamed up with the current administrative chief executive who holds a certificate in business language, specializing in French. Since export business involves a relatively high degree of interaction with various institutions within and outside the country, the respondents generally agreed that a minimum of formal education is required to start the business.

Previous Work Experience

The firms are most often established as second careers in the work history of the main proprietors. Nearly all of the owners have worked in either private enterprises (e.g., banks, manufacturing) or in public institutions (e.g., ministries and specialized public agencies). The founder and executive chairman of Kiku Company Limited comes from a position as deputy managing director of a state enterprise; Getrade's proprietor was the managing director of Johnson Wax, a subsidiary of an international detergent company; the proprietor of Combined Farmers had several years of managerial experience with Ghana Commercial Bank. They therefore bring to their own business not only rich professional experience but also a network of contacts with previous colleagues in both private and public organizations. It is generally acknowledged by the respondents that these contacts are exceedingly valuable sources of business information that help ease their interaction with the regulatory agencies of the macroenvironment.

SUMMARY

The Ghanaian nontraditional export subsector is characterized by the following features:

1. Dominance of family-owned, small-scale export firms is evident.
2. Most founders of these firms have good educational backgrounds, perhaps relatively higher than those in the nonexporting local firms.
3. Some of them operate several businesses simultaneously as a means of hedging against an economic downturn.

These features have important implications for the amount of resources and the managerial capacity that form the operational foundations of the export businesses. In line with the existing literature that presents managerial attitudes as a key determinant of export performance, it is necessary in this study to take a close look at the motives underlying the establishment of the export businesses themselves and the degree of commitment of their owners to the firms. These issues are explored in the next chapter.

Chapter 9

Initial Export Decisions and Their Underlying Motives

What motivates a small resource-deficient Ghanaian firm to initiate export transactions? How is the motivation sustained? How does such a firm overcome or compensate for its resource deficiencies? These are the key questions examined in this chapter. The discussion draws extensively upon the issues discussed in Part I.

EXPORT HISTORY OF THE FIRMS

Contrary to observations made in the Stages Models, nearly all the firms in this study had little or no domestic market experience in the products they export. As shown in Table 8.2, 55 percent of the firms started export sales in the same year as they were established or less than four years after their establishment. Thus, the firms were established as export businesses. For exporters of fresh food items, such as yams, the initial decision to enter business came from visits their founders made to North American and Western European countries where they discovered an unmet demand for these products, mainly among Ghanaian residents in these countries. The emergent strategy from such information was very simple: collect the products as they are, check for quality, package, and ship to distributors abroad on the basis of orders placed. Since the target consumers are Ghanaians, the markets abroad can be justifiably conceived as extensions of the domestic market, so no product adaptation is considered necessary. Furthermore, since the products have culture-specific and nostalgic value to the target consumers, they are willing to pay a premium for the opportunity to obtain them in their chosen countries of residence. This point is further discussed in Chapter 10 on market selection decisions.

EXPORT MOTIVES

Reasons given by respondents for entering into export business can be classified into four groups:

1. Acquisition of foreign currency to finance ongoing import businesses
2. Acquisition of foreign currency to finance other investments
3. Lack of (or declining) domestic demand for the firm's products
4. Growth/expansion of the operations of the firm

Foreign Currency Demand As an Export Motive

Table 9.1 provides an overview of the motives given by firms in the four product categories. Foreign exchange acquisition dominates the motives for exporting nonprocessed food items. Only

TABLE 9.1. Export Motives/Categories of Firms

Export motives	Non-processed food items		Processed food items		Nonfood raw materials		Light manufac-tures		Total	
	No.	%	No.	%	No.	%	No.	%	No.	%
Acquiring foreign currency to finance import businesses	3	15	—	—	1	5	—	—	4	20
Acquiring foreign currency to finance other investments	3	15	—	—	1	5	2	10	6	30
Lack of/decline in domestic demand for products	—	—	—	—	—	—	2	10	2	10
Growth/expansion	3	15	2	10	—	—	3	15	8	40
Total	9	45	2	10	2	10	7	35	20	100

one-third of this category gave "growth" as a primary export motive; two-thirds were motivated by foreign exchange acquisition. The two firms in the sample that export nonfood raw materials (cattle horn and cottonseed) also do so for reasons of foreign exchange (see Baah-Nuakoh et al., 1996, for similar evidence).

In contrast, the two firms exporting processed food items (fruit juice and beer) gave market growth as their main motive for engaging in export business. Three of the seven exporters of light manufactures subscribed to the same motive, while two (Scanstyle Limited and Spintex Limited) gave domestic market conditions as their motives. Only two exporters within this product category had foreign exchange as a motive.

The explanations for the preponderance of foreign exchange as an export motive in Ghana may be found in the diversity in small-scale entrepreneurs' lines of business, as well as several decades of foreign currency constraint. Nearly 50 percent of the nonprocessed food exporters are engaged in other lines of business (imports, construction, etc.). The same holds true for the two firms exporting nonfood raw materials as well as the exporter of carved wooden doors (Woody Limited). For owners of the firms, exporting provides them with a greater opportunity to acquire the foreign currency they need to import equipment or items they require in their other lines of business.

According to the marketing literature, diversification growth makes sense when good opportunities can be found outside current main lines of business. Good opportunity here refers to a business situation that is attractive and for which the focal firm has the mix of business strengths needed to be successful. The entry barriers for the nonprocessed food export businesses are very low. With good contacts abroad, a flair for trading, as well as good educational background and tolerance to maneuver through the jungle of administrative procedures, a businessperson can fairly easily enter this line of business. Thus, for those already in import business, exporting nonprocessed food items provides a good business opportunity, especially since the foreign exchange so gained strengthens their positions in the import sector.

Such a diversification may produce macroeconomic growth if exporters engage in the production of the food items themselves rather than buying them from the peasant farmers. The fragmented nature of peasant farming in Ghana reduces the sector's capacity to take advantage of increased demand for food items by increasing investment and thereby food supply. The available data from this study do not produce conclusive evidence of the investment intentions of the entrepreneurs. So far, none of the firms selling fresh foodstuffs, such as yams, have any specific plans for entering into farming. They are willing to assist the local farmers by providing them with short-term credit facilities to cover their immediate farming expenses but are reluctant to enter into an enduring and deeply committed relationship with them.

In light of this observation, conventional measures of export performance are inappropriate for the assessment of the operations of these firms. Since gains from other businesses in which the entrepreneurs are involved depend to a substantial extent on the foreign currency at their disposal, managers of these firms assess their export performance more in terms of the net gains in foreign currency than volume and value of sales. As long as the export transactions provide a net foreign currency to support the other businesses, the managers may view their performance as satisfactory. Local currency earnings from these other businesses may be sufficient to justify managers' export transactions. It is therefore doubtful if they will commit their time and resources exclusively to the export business.

Domestic Market Conditions As an Export Trigger

As noted earlier, two of the firms producing light manufactures indicated that domestic market conditions triggered their decision to enter the export business. One of the firms, Scanstyle Limited, produces and exports furniture, furniture parts, as well as parquet floors and panels for the building industry. Exports constitute 95 percent of the firm's total sales, and its products are sold mainly to customers in the United Kingdom, Ireland, Denmark, Italy, and Germany. Although this firm was established in 1968, it has sold only a limited quantity of its products on the domestic market, largely due to the low income level in the country. Naturally, Scanstyle's organizational structure and business strategy reflect a strong commitment to exports. The company has created an export department whose manager reports directly to the managing director. A unit under this department is located in the United Kingdom, with a European sales representative in charge. The major tasks of this unit include securing orders, monitoring the market, and liaising with customers.

The other company, Spintex Limited, produces textiles, including Ghanaian traditional cloth, *kente*.[1] Similar to many other manufacturing firms in Ghana, Spintex has been grappling with problems of declining domestic sales as a result of the liberalization of imports in Ghana and the general fall in demand engendered by the structural adjustment program. Spintex's low competitive position on the domestic market against imports from Southeast Asian countries is attributable to the fact that the firm relies on imported raw materials and utilizes only 50 percent of its production capacity, with a labor force of 800 workers. Through exports of specialized products, such as *kente* cloth, to Ghanaians abroad, Spintex expects to increase its capacity utilization and minimize average unit cost of production. This will hopefully improve its competitive position on the domestic market as well.

Although the two companies entered the export business largely motivated by domestic market conditions, the strength of their motivation appears to be different. As indicated earlier, Scanstyle shows a fairly high degree of commitment to the export business because it has no domestic market to fall back on. It is doubtful if Spintex has the same degree of commitment to its internationalization process. The company has no separate export department and sells to only a limited market segment of Ghanaians in the United States. Management has expressed interest in exploring opportunities within similar market segments in Europe but has no definite plans. For firms such as Spintex, the temptation to withdraw from export markets is very potent and must be expected once the domestic market begins to pick up again.

Our doubts regarding the commitment of some Ghanaian manufacturing firms to export business must also be viewed in light of the domestic economy's impact on these firms' competitive capacities. As Goodwin (1993) argues, there is continuous pressure on firms in the private sectors of the developing economies to reduce costs by lowering product quality. This enables them to offer the products at affordable prices to the predominantly low-income consumers. However, this quality reduction undermines the firms' motivation to invest in improved technology and to undertake other productivity improvement activities, thereby eroding its competitive positions in foreign markets. Thus, although Spintex expects export business to improve its overall competitive position, it has so far been able to sell only one unique product, *kente,* with a very restrictive demand abroad. In recent years, the African-American population in the United States has adopted *kente* as a symbol of racial identity. This perhaps opens up new market opportunities that firms such as Spintext can exploit.

Growth As an Export Motive

It is remarkable to note that 40 percent of the respondents indicated "growth" as their primary motivation for export (see Table 9.1). This group includes three exporters of nonprocessed food items (shea nut, shrimp, and pineapple), two processed food exporters (fruit juice and beer), and three producers/exporters of light manufactures and handicrafts. A distinctive characteristic of these firms is that they are relatively larger than all the others in the sample, in terms of number of employees, volume of output, and levels of investment. The pineapple, shrimp, and fruit juice exporting firms have assets of about ten, twenty, and thirty million U.S. dollars, respectively. All of them employ over 250 workers and are the front-runners within their respective industries.

Beer exports are undertaken by the country's first and leading brewery, Accra Brewery, which was established in 1931 and employs over 500 workers. The profile of the producers of the light manufactures is the same. Poly Products is among the few manufacturing firms in Ghana using brand-new technology and whose management assesses the company's financial standing to be strong. The firm employs 225 workers, and its products are in high demand in the domestic market. Similarly, Packrite Industries and Poly Products have recently moved into a new factory, with new equipment financed partly by funds from the International Finance Corporation (IFC) and the Standard Chartered Bank. Thus, these firms have a solid operational foundation in the domestic market and relatively good bases for competing in the regional market.

The available evidence suggests that growth as an export motive is associated with firm size, measured in terms of assets and number of employees. Unlike the firms who state foreign exchange acquisition as their overriding objective, growth-oriented firms have solid financial bases for their businesses and are in good standing with both foreign and local banks. Their chances of marshaling sufficient financial resources for their businesses are therefore very bright.

For some of the firms, the growth motive can be partly explained by the nonavailability of substantial domestic demand for the products they sell, for example, shea nut and shrimp. For others, however, growth through exports is a proactive strategy, since the domestic market for these products is significant (e.g., beer and packaging items) and over 90 percent of their sales are made in this market.

EXPORT MOTIVES REEXAMINED

The evidence that has been discussed is not entirely consistent with the expectations of firm behavior suggested in the Stages Models of internationalization. As noted earlier, the initial export decision is mainly proactive and based on owner-managers' aspirations and expectations. However, the influence of government promotional initiatives plays an important role in the realizations of the export ambitions of individual managers. This point is developed further when we discuss the institutional context of the export business in Chapter 11. It is sufficient to note at this point, that exporters' ability to find markets for their products depends largely on the customer-linking initiatives of the promotional agencies.

The proactive orientation of these firms may be due mainly to the nature of their products. Unsolicited orders can hardly be expected for traditional Ghanaian fresh food items such as yams. Furthermore, since Ghana is unknown in key markets as a producer of fresh fruits and other nontraditional raw materials, such as shea nuts and animal products, exporters of these items must make themselves known to potential importers/foreign customers. The evidence here is therefore consistent with points made in our theoretical discussions in Chapter 1.

Exporters of light manufactures appear to be in a situation that approximates the assumptions in the Stages Models. Firms producing packaging materials (e.g., Packrite Industries and Poly Products) sell to industrial customers (i.e., other firms) within the domestic market. The recent upsurge in economic activities in Ghana has resulted in significant increases in the demand for their products. Thus, export markets are not an immediate major interest. Their only deliberate export-related activities are participation in local trade fairs and exhibitions as well as registration with export promotion institutions. The orders they have filled from neighboring countries are largely unsolicited. Nevertheless, their managers have a vision of growing into these markets and are willing to use their current limited involvement as a means of gaining market knowledge and operational experience.

SUMMARY

The evidence discussed in this chapter shows that Ghanaian exporting firms tend to have little or no domestic market experience prior to their decisions to embark on exports. Three main motives influence their export decision:

1. Foreign currency acquisition
2. Growth/expansion of existing businesses
3. Lack of or decrease in domestic demand for their products

The prominence of foreign currency acquisition as a motive can be explained by the several decades of foreign currency shortage in Ghana. As noted in Chapter 7, the Ghanaian government has introduced a foreign currency retention scheme as part of its export incentive package. Judging from the evidence, the scheme has addressed an important need among Ghanaian businesspeople and will continue to be popular as long as the country continues to face foreign currency shortages.

Chapter 10

Market Knowledge Generation, Market Selection, and Entry Mode Decisions of Ghanaian Firms

As discussed in Chapter 1, the existing literature suggests that most exporting firms start their internationalization by selling to geographically close and culturally similar markets and expanding successively into markets with greater differences in physical and cultural characteristics. The incremental process of internationalization allows firms to acquire market knowledge and export experience gradually to reduce uncomfortable surprises in their operations abroad. The firms covered in this study are relatively small, lack resources, and initiate their export activities immediately or a few years after their establishment so it would benefit them to start their operations in the aforementioned manner to gain needed knowledge and experience. This chapter therefore examines how the firms acquire knowledge about their target markets, how they decide which markets to enter, and what related channel decisions they make.

MARKET INFORMATION AND APPROACHES TO MARKET KNOWLEDGE ACQUISITION

Contrary to the view expressed in the Stages Models, Ghanaian exporters are usually vigorously involved in market search prior to their first export order. These searches, however, do not take the form prescribed in the existing literature; that is, they do not engage in collection and analysis of elaborate market information to arrive at their decisions. Table 10.1 presents evidence of the means by which the firms secured their market information and first export orders.

TABLE 10.1. Methods of Acquiring Initial Export Orders/Categories of Firms

Methods	Non-processed food items No.	%	Processed food items No.	%	Nonfood raw materials No.	%	Light manufac-tures No.	%	Total No.	%
Through friends/ contacts abroad	1	5	—	—	1	5	1	5	3	15
Through GEPC*-sponsored exhibi-tions	1	5	—	—	1	5	5	25	7	35
Business trips abroad	6	30	—	—	—	—	1	5	7	35
Unsolicited orders	1	5	2	10	—	—	—	—	3	15
Total	9	45	2	10	2	10	7	35	20	100

* GEPC = Ghana Export Promotion Council

Evidently, visits abroad and contacts made during trade fairs and exhibitions provided the firms with the information they required to make their initial export decisions. Of the companies, 70 percent secured their first export orders through these means, 15 percent relied on enquiries made by foreign customers, and another 15 percent relied on information given to them by friends. In general, these findings are in agreement with the study by Baah-Nuakoh and colleagues (1996, p. 67), with one exception: They found that most Ghanaian exporters obtained their first export order by being approached by a foreign buyer, i.e., unsolicited orders, in our terminology. The explanation may be that the many exporters from the traditional sector in the Baah-Nuakoh study face proactive global sources (see Chapter 12).

The role of export-facilitating institutions such as the Ghana Export Promotion Council (GEPC), the Ghana Chamber of Commerce (GCC), and specialized product associations in linking the firms with prospective customers abroad has been repeatedly emphasized by those interviewed. Many importers make their first contacts with these local institutions in search of specific products that they believe can be obtained in Ghana. Since nearly all reputable exporting firms are registered with these institutions, they are linked to the prospective importers. This, in some cases, becomes the start of enduring trading relationships with respective importers.

A further breakdown of the data shows that exporters of nonprocessed food items rely mainly on business trips abroad as a source of market information. Exporters of light manufactures, on the other hand, rely mainly on contacts made at trade fairs and exhibitions. The difference in orientation is possibly due to the nature of the products and their target markets. Nonprocessed food items, being perishable, are not items for exhibitions; thus, potential customers are rarely found at the trade fairs. Furthermore, as subsequent evidence indicates, these items are sold mainly in Europe and North America, either to migrant Ghanaians (in the case of yams) or to fruit dealers (in the case of fresh pineapples). The normal practice for small-scale exporters of such products is to identify specific agents or customers and negotiate directly with them. Once exports to a particular market were initiated, the exporter and importer paid business visits to each other to monitor activities and confirm/strengthen relations. In a number of cases, however, it was observed that the Ghanaian exporter was rather inactive when it came to visiting and monitoring the export markets.

The nature of light manufactures, such as aluminium plates, makes them amenable to presentation at fairs and exhibitions, both in neighboring West African countries and in Europe. Again, the promotional initiatives of the GEPC have encouraged managers to participate in such trade exhibitions and to use the council as a major source of market information. Thus, the owner of Woody Limited, a crafted-door exporter, started his internationalization process by retailing a few doors to customers who visited the trade fairs and exhibitions in which he participated. Luckily, during an exhibition in Germany, one of these customers introduced him to an importer of wood products who placed an order for a few doors on a trial basis. This marked the beginning of his export business. Similarly, Packrite Industries (exporting cartons) and Poly Products Limited (exporting polythene bags) were contacted by importers from Togo at trade exhibitions in Ghana. Both companies have since made sporadic exports to Togo and Côte d'Ivoire and have used these transactions as avenues for collecting market information.

Since the business community in Ghana is relatively small and exporters are concentrated in the Accra-Tema metropolitan area, business owners and top executives tend to socialize together, i.e., belong to the same social clubs and business organizations. Contacts made with business friends during such club or association meetings serve as a vital source of market information. Thus, the owner-manager of Woody Limited, specifically, stated that some of his market leads were received from his "fellows" in the Lions Club, an international social organization with a branch in Ghana.

In a few cases, the customer search/analysis proceeds in a systematic, rational manner. Some firms make a cursory review of lists of importers of the products in which they deal and select some for initial contacts through business trips to the countries in which they are located. Thus, the managing director of Kiku Company Limited approached KLM Airline for data on shrimp distributors in the Netherlands, with the understanding that the airline is likely to be a major carrier of shrimp entering the Netherlands. He obtained the data and short-listed some of the distributors for contact. Subsequently, however, he acted on a "tip" from one of his friends to contact a distributor who was not included in the list of distributors that he had obtained from KLM. He went to meet the distributor personally, and their discussions resulted in a business relationship that he describes as "reciprocally rewarding and trustworthy."

Thus, even when systematic market investigations are attempted, the mediation of a friend in the market search may be highly critical in the decision-making process of Ghanaian exporters. A friend's recommendation appears more reliable and therefore carries more weight than the data that may be available. This is also illustrated by the example of Getrade Limited, an exporter of handicrafts. The managing director decided to enter the German market with his first exports on the advice of a German friend whom he subsequently employed as his export manager. The managing director of Combined Farmers secured his first export order with similar assistance.

In summary, the evidence presented here suggests that most Ghanaian exporters behave as variants of the Action Man and the Networker decision makers introduced in Chapter 2. As argued earlier, these types find market research a less relevant approach to market knowledge acquisition due to their limited experience on which to base such analysis. Visits to target markets to meet with potential customers provide them with a more reliable or psychologically satisfactory means of reducing their uncertainties about the markets.

With regard to networking, information is acquired through two principal sources:

1. Contacts with friends and relatives in target markets, some of whom may be prospective customers
2. Contacts with foreigners in Ghana, some of whom may be interested in dealing in the products in question

Some of these contacts have been rather coincidental and do not provide sustainable sources of market information. In situations in which the foreigner acts as an exporting firm or an outsourcer, the Ghanaian firm gains limited market knowledge and is therefore vulnerable to opportunistic maneuvers by the latter. Where the foreigner becomes an employee (as in the case of the German export manager in Getrade Limited) he or she provides the firm with valuable market knowledge for the commencement of the export business.

CHOICE OF MARKETS

Part of the empirical evidence from this study goes against the conventional perception that firms start their internationalization process by exporting to nearby, culturally similar markets. As shown in Table 10.2, 65 percent of the firms report exporting their products mainly to Western Europe, 60 percent of the firms sell to other African customers, while 40 percent export to North America. This pattern of export direction is consistent with evidence from a broader analysis of the nontraditional export subsector conducted by the GEPC (1995). As shown in a recent analysis, nearly 63 percent of all nontraditional exports in 1995 went to European Union member countries (mainly the United Kingdom, France, Germany, Belgium, Italy, the Netherlands, and Spain). Other developed countries and the ECOWAS countries received 17 percent.

TABLE 10.2. Major Trading Countries/Categories of Firms

Countries	Non-processed food items		Processed food items		Nonfood raw materials		Light manufac-tures		Total	
	No.	%	No.	%	No.	%	No.	%	No.	%
Western Europe	6	30	1	5	1	5	5	25	13	65
Africa	3	15	1	5	—	—	8	40	12	60
North America	3	15	1	5	—	—	4	20	8	40
Asia	2	10	—	—	2	10	—	—	4	20

A further breakdown of the data shows that the firms do not limit their exports to a single market (see Table 10.3). Fifteen of the firms export to two or more markets, with only five exporting to a single market. Each firm, however, has one key market that the owner visits frequently. The other markets are only occasionally served.

Markets for Nonprocessed and Processed Food Items

Turning to each specific product category, it can be noted that seven (of the nine) firms exporting nonprocessed food items choose to sell them in West European countries, mainly the United Kingdom, Switzerland, the Netherlands, Germany, and Italy (see Table 10.4). One firm exports yams to the United States (in addition to the

TABLE 10.3. Number of Countries to Which Exports Are Sold

Number	Non-processed food items No.	Processed food items No.	Nonfood raw materials No.	Light manufac-tures No.	Total No.	Total %
Only 1 country	3	—	—	2	5	25
2-3 countries	4	2	1	1	8	40
More than 3 countries	2	—	1	4	7	35
Total	9	2	2	7	20	100

TABLE 10.4. Major Trading Regions for Firms Exporting Nonprocessed Food Items

Items	Western Europe	North America	Africa
Fresh pineapples	2	—	—
Yams	2	1	—
Kola nuts	—	—	1
Shea nuts	1	—	—
Cashew nuts	1	—	—
Common salt	—	—	1
Shrimp	1	—	—
Total	7	1	2
Percent	70	10	20

Note: Figures indicate the number of firms exporting to each region.

United Kingdom). Common salt is sold to customers in landlocked West African countries such as Mali, Burkina Faso, and Niger. The kola nuts exporter deals with importers in Nigeria who subsequently reexport the nuts to Europe. This evidence again is consistent with the national pattern as reported in a 1995 GEPC analysis.

A plausible explanation for these market choices may be found in the nature of products carried by the firms and their demand characteristics. Considering the nonprocessed food category, our findings are that exported yams are purchased primarily by West African and Caribbean residents abroad and are therefore exported to countries with relatively heavy concentrations of migrant Africans, e.g., the United States, the United Kingdom, and Germany. Since these products are grown in the neighboring countries and Ghana has no significant comparative advantage in their production compared to other West African countries, the latter cannot constitute a viable export market for yams. The lack of comparative advantage also holds true for fresh pineapples, which grow relatively well in several West African countries, including Ghana's neighboring country, Côte d'Ivoire.

The results of this study corroborate evidence from other African countries. For example, Jaffee (1993) notes that a large majority of Kenya's horticultural export trade has been directed to Western Europe, especially to the United Kingdom. The close macroeconomic and political ties between Kenya and the United Kingdom, the relatively extensive air traffic between the two countries, as well as the fact that many Kenyans have lived, worked, and/or studied in the United Kingdom combine to reduce the informational barriers between the two countries, thereby facilitating market entry for small Kenyan exporters.

The decision of Ghanaian and other African firms to sell fresh pineapples to European customers is reinforced by the fact that these countries represent the world's leading import markets for fresh fruits as well as fruit and vegetable juices. Fifteen of the twenty leading import markets of pineapple juice listed in the International Trade Center (ITC) market study of 1991 were all West European.

As noted previously, only two of the twenty firms in this study export processed food products (fruit juice and beer). Fruit juice is exported mainly to Libya as a result of bilateral trade arrangements between the Libyan and Ghanaian governments. Some of the products, however, find their way to the neighboring countries of Côte d'Ivoire and Togo through the efforts of petty traders engaged in cross-border trading. Astek Limited, however, is not fully aware of the volume of this trade and has no immediate ambition of exploring these markets through direct export arrangements.

Markets for Light Manufactures

Table 10.5 provides a breakdown of the market choices of the seven firms engaged in export activities. Furniture parts and other wood products are sold in Western Europe (the United Kingdom, Ireland, Denmark) and the United States.

Packaging materials such as cartons and polythene bags are sold in the neighboring countries of Côte d'Ivoire and Togo. The same goes for aluminium products. Textile products have the same target market groups as yams and beer from Ghana and are therefore sold in European and North American countries with relatively high concentrations of Africans.

The market selection decisions of firms that export packaging materials and aluminium products tend to follow the expectations of the Learning Stages Theory discussed in Chapter 1. As explained

TABLE 10.5. Major Trading Regions for Firms Exporting Light Manufactures

Items	Western Europe	North America	Africa
Furniture and other wood products	1	1	—
Packaging materials	—	—	2
Aluminum products	—	—	1
Textiles	—	1	—
Craft and artisan products	1	1	—
Total	2	3	3

earlier, the neighboring country, Togo was the first export market for both firms. Poly Products Limited, has subsequently entered Côte d'Ivoire as its second export market. Exports are still sporadic because the domestic market remains not fully satisfied. Unlike the food exporters, the good financial standing of both firms means that the acquisition of foreign currency is not a strong motive for exporting.

EXPORTERS' PERCEPTIONS OF THE SELECTED MARKETS

A fundamental question raised by this evidence is whether Ghanaian exporters perceive these geographically distant markets as culturally unfamiliar to them. Evidently, the final consumers of yams in Germany and the United States share common cultural foundations with the exporters, being Ghanaians themselves. Exports to these market segments can be considered an extension of the domestic market. This argument is further reinforced by the fact that the distributors are migrant Ghanaians. The degree of uncertainty associated with such transactions is limited. Furthermore, our discussion of the demographic profile of the proprietors and managers of these firms suggests that Western Europe and North America are fairly familiar to most of them, through either previous business activities as importers or previous employment or education in these countries. They may therefore perceive these markets and channel systems as more familiar to them than the geographically close markets. Many of the managers interviewed believe that doing business with European customers is a lot easier than doing business across African borders, simply because the former involves an established tradition for importing and the actors are more familiar with the rules of the game. Frequently cited evidence in support of this view is the difficulties encountered by exporters to neighboring African countries in receiving payments for the goods they sell.

Furthermore, the evidence from this project does not validate the dominant assumption that geographical proximity increases the probability of countries sharing common business cultures. A critical dimension in the discussion of business cultures (apparently ignored in the existing literature) is the impact of historical, international political relations on the development of business cultures. The history of colonization of the West African countries has resulted in their division into two distinctive business zones, the English zone, including Ghana, Sierra Leone, Liberia, and Nigeria, and the Francophone zone, composed of the other countries in the region. The latter group of countries has adopted a modified version of business regulations and procedures found in France, combined with the vestiges of Arab influence from previous contacts with Arab merchants. To this is added a generous dose of their own cultural rules of behavior. The former English colonies, naturally, have adopted versions of English business rules and procedures along with their own cultural prescriptions.

The differences between regulations and business cultures in Ghana and the Francophone countries have created major invisible trade barriers for firms exporting to Togo, Niger, and Burkina Faso. One invisible trade barrier is the problems associated with receiving payments for goods supplied to cross-border customers. The Francophone countries have no national currencies of their own. They belong to two monetary unions whose common denominator is the currency known as the CFA Franc. Due to special arrangements with France, the CFA Franc is a convertible currency. Consequently, importers' distributors in the Francophone countries channel payments for their imports from Ghana through French banks that in turn transfer them through English banks before they arrive in Ghana.

There are also problems with trans–West African logistics. Respondents who export to West African countries complained that vehicles of certain sizes and weights are allowed to use Ghanaian roads but are not allowed on roads in the Francophone countries. These countries demand physical inspection of all items on the vehicles, thereby causing delays in the transportation of goods. This situation often causes firms to indulge in corrupt practices to get their goods to their customers on schedule, and such corruption substantially increases the cost of export products. Coupled with this are the protracted political disputes between Ghana and Togo that have resulted in frequent closures of the borders between the two countries.

It can be argued, however, that were the markets well developed and the channel systems functioning properly, collaborative efforts would have been possible between the suppliers and their customers in the respective countries to exert pressure on the political institutions to minimize these problems.

CHANNEL DECISIONS AND ENTRY STRATEGIES

Channel members are called several different names in the conventional literature, which makes it generally difficult to identify a specific type of middleman merely by name. This difficulty has been aggravated in this study because respondents' choices of terminology differed and did not conform to the terms normally found in the literature.

Categories of Middlemen

The classification in Table 10.6 follows the respondents' usage of the terms. They use the term "middlemen" to cover different categories of marketing intermediaries with whom they deal. These include wholesalers who import directly from them or agents who act on behalf of wholesalers or major retailers. A few sell directly to big stores and supermarkets, such as Sainsbury in the United Kingdom and JCPenney in the United States.

As indicated in Table 10.6, over 50 percent of the firms sell to importers or overseas agents. The importers function either as

TABLE 10.6. Exporters' Choice of Channel Members

Middlemen	Non-processed food items	Processed food items	Nonfood raw materials	Light manufac-tures	Total
Importers/ overseas agents	9	—	2	—	11
Import retailers	2	1	—	1	4
Local agents	—	1	—	2	3

Note: Three companies (light manufacturers) sold directly to customers.

wholesalers or retailers. Food items such as pineapples, which are earmarked for a broader segment of consumers, are sold to import wholesalers who, in turn, sell to supermarkets and other retailers. The culture-specific food items, such as yams, are sold to import retailers, who either sell them to regular customers on a mail-order basis (where customers are geographically dispersed within the given country) or through speciality stores. Some of the yam traders may function as wholesalers to a few retail shops within the importing country. Two of the yam exporters specifically indicated that they exported to import retailers in particular countries.

The retail channel system, which is used by handicraft exporters, deserves special attention. In several Western European countries, a number of alternative retail units have been established by political activists who are favorably disposed toward third world countries and have poverty alleviation high on their political agendas. They purchase artisan products at higher than local market prices and appeal to target customers with similar political inclinations. Getrade Limited, the major handicraft exporter in this study, exports its products to such retailers in Germany, Switzerland, and the Netherlands.

Similar to yams, *kente* textiles are either sold directly to customers or through importers/retailers. Wood products, such as doors, furniture parts, and parquet flooring, are sold directly to building companies that order them through the overseas sales offices of the exporting firms or to a few individuals who visit the companies' exhibitions at trade fairs in Ghana or abroad.

Channel Risk and Management

It is doubtful whether these middlemen are deliberately chosen on the basis of a rational assessment made by the Ghanaian exporters. The general impression conveyed during the interviews was that the channel options were rather few and some of the exporters had no real choices, partly because their small size and export volumes make them less attractive to bigger overseas importers/ distributors. This weakens their bargaining position and raises the probability of some of them falling prey to the opportunistic inclinations of import merchants.

Lack of market knowledge and export experience as well as resource limitations impose additional constraints on their choices. Naturally, by selling through the smaller middlemen, the exporters have relinquished control over marketing strategies and processes for their products. Selling fresh food items on the European and North American markets, in particular, poses serious channel problems. These markets tend to feature oligopolistic structures at import as well as wholesale/distributor levels (Jaffee, 1993). The multiple chain supermarkets, which increasingly dominate the retail markets for these commodities, are fed from these highly concentrated wholesale outlets. It is not unusual for the distributors to own the supermarkets.

As suggested in the Network Theory discussed in Chapter 1, a new entrant into such a tightly structured distribution system faces severe drawbacks, especially if the firm is small and, therefore, competitively weak. Foreign agents or importers with whom exporters deal on an occasional basis are likely to exhibit opportunistic tendencies, taking advantage of the fact that the products are perishable and the exporters do not have any means of getting immediate information about market trends in the importing countries. Examples of agents misreporting actual sales results, misinforming the exporter about overall market conditions, or reporting deterioration of the quality of the products in transit have been given by the respondents. Such distortions in market information naturally undermine the firms' ability to design marketing strategies that can enhance their competitive position.

MARKET SPREAD AND GROWTH POTENTIALS

Distinction is usually drawn in the export marketing literature between market concentration and market spreading as strategic options. Market concentration strategy implies that the exporting firm focuses on a small number of key markets and develops a strong position in them before venturing into new markets. The advantage of this approach is that the amount of resources spent in controlling and coordinating international transactions (relative to volume of exports) is lower. However, in situations in which the markets are selected on the basis of initial responses to customers' orders, it is doubtful whether these markets provide the firm with the best export opportunities. If the firm decides not to enter new markets despite unfavorable performance in the existing markets, this may reflect management's aversion to risk or complacency at lower performance levels.

The available evidence from this study reflects the general tendency among Ghanaian firms to concentrate their operations in a few markets. On the average, the firms export to two markets or derive about 80 percent of their export earnings from one or two markets. The prospects of market expansion tend to be constrained by two principal factors: (1) the nature of the demand for the products exported and (2) relationships developed with current distributors of the products. As mentioned previously, the demand for such products as yams and *kente* (the consumption of which is culture specific) is restricted to Ghanaian communities abroad, so the products are exported only to countries with relatively large concentrations of Ghanaians. Exporters of these products can only adopt strategies that aim at furthering the degree of penetration of the existing markets, e.g., increasing the number of Ghanaians buying the products in each country as well as the number of purchases they make. Exporters interviewed are very optimistic about their prospects of increasing sales in these countries, provided other constraints (see Perceived Problems and Coping Strategies in Chapter 11) can be removed.

Products such as handicrafts, fresh pineapples, and processed tropical fruit juices have greater potential for market expansion since product demand is not limited to Ghanaian residents abroad. However, their exporters face serious supply constraints that make them unattractive trading partners for large-scale distributors in the industrialized countries. Thus, Astek Limited (the tropical fruit juice exporter) had to turn down orders from Danish distributors because the demand volumes exceeded the firm's existing production capacity. Similarly, Baah-Nuakoh and colleagues (1996) report that over 50 percent of their respondents have, at one time, declined export orders due to capacity limitations. As Olsen, Biswas, and Kacker (1992) argue, European customers expect suppliers from the developing countries to show evidence of their capacity to fulfill delivery obligations. It is therefore safer for firms that are in doubt of their own delivery capacities to decline orders rather than making promises that they are unlikely to fulfill satisfactorily.

The firms appear, however, to show some reluctance in conducting active searches for new markets, even for products with market spread potential. Once a firm has found a fairly reliable distributor in its initial export market, it expects the distributor to undertake subsequent market expansion on its behalf. Kiku Company Limited, for example, has assessed the European market to be generally suitable for its products. Nevertheless, the firm has relied on a Dutch distributor, Denheijer, to sell its products within the European Union market and has no control over the marketing strategies adopted by that firm. Similarly, Combined Farmers started its export business supplying 100 cartons of pineapples to a distributor in Switzerland with whom the managing director was linked through a friend. Since then new distributors have been found in the United Kingdom, Belgium, and Italy. However, none of them has proved reliable, so the firm's market expansion has been limited.

In situations in which the initial importer/distributor proves unreliable, the firm's continued presence and subsequent penetration into that market will depend on its ability to disengage from its current relationship and find new importers/distributors for its products or adopt measures that improve its ability to supervise the marketing process. Where no enforceable contractual relationships exist between the firm and its current distributor, a switch to another distributor is less problematic. Where the supplier is attractive and the channel system is highly competitive, finding a new importer/distributor will not pose a major problem. If the reverse is true, however, switching to a new channel member becomes a less attractive option. In general, it was found that Ghanaian exporters tended to stick to their first choice of distributor, even if it subsequently turned out not to provide them with a continuous stream of orders.

SUMMARY

In summary, the evidence shows that Ghanaian exporters rely heavily on government export promotion institutions (e.g., the GEPC) and business trips abroad to obtain information about export opportunities. Foreigners living in Ghana as well as Ghanaians living abroad also serve as sources of information about prospective importers. With respect to market choice, most exporters of food items target their products at customers in Western Europe and North America where market opportunities are assessed to be good. Exporters of light manufactures, however, sell to customers in neighboring countries. The difference in the directions of exports of these two categories of products can be explained by the competitive advantages that the products have in the various markets. It has been argued that climatic conditions provide Ghanaian producers a comparative advantage over North American and European farmers in the production of tropical food items such as tropical fruits and vegetables. Thus, these products are exported mainly to Europe and North America. Light manufactures, on the other hand, are exported mainly to neighboring West African countries where Ghanaian producers appear to have good competitive positions.

Chapter 11

Assessment of the Institutional Context of Export Businesses

The Contingency and (Inter)Action Models discussed in Chapter 1 suggest that a firm's internationalization process cannot be fully understood outside the institutional context or environment within which its operations are embedded. The institutions that affect a firm's operation may be many and may differ markedly in terms of their objectives, modes of operation, levels of authority, forms of organization, as well as attitudes and habits of their staff. For these institutions to have an optimum impact on the behavior of firms, they must be perceived by the firms to be supportive. This is because it is the perception of managers that influences their behavior. As argued by Czinkota and Ricks (1994), problems that management can handle easily are not perceived to be significant, although they recur frequently, while less frequent problems may be perceived as burdensome, despite their occasional occurrence, simply because management has not found a good means of handling them. This chapter therefore focuses attention on perception rather than offering any objective assessment of the gravity of problems created or solved by public institutions during the course of export transaction.

AN OVERVIEW OF THE INSTITUTIONAL CONTEXT

Two types of institutions have been identified as relevant for the purposes of this study: public and private institutions. The former category includes all government and (quasi)governmental institutions that directly or indirectly affect the operations of Ghanaian firms, in general, and/or export firms, in particular. The latter category refers to those institutions other than firms that are established by industries to perform specific tasks or to facilitate the general development of the sector. The private institutions covered in the study include the Federation of Association of Ghanaian Exporters (FAGE) as well as the various product associations established under its umbrella. Fourteen product associations were in operation in 1995 (Tetteh, 1996). The formation of these associations is indicative of the exporting firms' desire to collaborate in the development of their businesses and to create an avenue for dialogue with (quasi)governmental institutions such as the Ghana Export Promotion Council and the Trade Fairs Authority.

Viewed from a functional perspective, the government institutions may be classified in three categories:

1. *Promotional institutions* that are purposely established to create incentives and facilities that motivate firms to engage in exporting
2. *Facilitatory institutions* whose actions directly or indirectly enhance the operational capabilities of firms
3. *Regulatory institutions* to ensure that firms provide the goods and services promised and that their behaviors, in general, conform with established standards in the country and/or abroad

The functions of the institutions are, however, not always neatly delineated in practice. For example, regulatory institutions may perform facilitatory and/or promotional services to mitigate any unintended negative consequences that their main activities may have for the development of the firms. Thus, the Customs, Excise, and Preventive Services (CEPS) in Ghana administers the duty drawback scheme that allows for a refund of duties paid on imports that are reexported or on imported inputs used in the production of exports. Similarly, some facilitatory institutions may add promotional dimensions to their main activities or collaborate with other institutions to do the same. Table 11.1 provides an idea of the types of institutions involved in the nontraditional export sector development process in Ghana.

TABLE 11.1. Institutional Context and Export Support Scheme in Ghana (December 1995)

Name of Institution	Type of Institution	Type of Scheme	Main Content of Scheme
Ghana Export Promotion Council (GEPC)	Promotional	Export promotion	To ensure the success of the national export diversification drive through an extensive scope of activities.
Private Enterprise and Export Development (PEED)	Facilitatory	Export finance	To promote the growth of private Ghanaian exporters through the provision of short-term credits to exporters and the provision of technical assistance.
Africa Project Development Facility (APDF)	Facilitatory/ promotional	Advisory services	To prepare feasibility studies and help enterpreneurs to secure financing from banks and appropriate sources of funds.
Customs, Excise, and Preventive Services (CEPS)	Regulatory	Duty drawback	Refund of duties, etc., paid on imports that are used in producing export articles.
International Executive Service Corps (IESC)	Facilitatory	Executive services	Provides individual firms with volunteer executive industry specialists for periods ranging from two to six months.
Trade and Investment Program (TIP-Ghana)	Facilitatory	Institutional support services	Influences changes in official policies that hinder exports; removes confusing rules and regulations, bottlenecks, such as documentation in exporting.
Techoserve	Facilitatory	Production and marketing assistance	Assists small-scale farmers and farmers' cooperatives in production, management, and marketing.
Ghana Investment Promotion Centre (GIPC)	Promotional	Investment promotion	Attracts foreign investors and encourages local investors through the creation of favorable conditions.
Ghana National Chamber of Commerce (GNCC)	Facilitatory/ promotional	Information and relational services	Enhances international trade opportunities through information and contacts.
Trade Promotion Unit (TPU) of Ministry of Trade and Industry (MOTI)	Facilitatory/ promotional	Trade promotion	Policy formulation, regulations, and resolution of export trade problems.
Export Finance Company (EFC)	Facilitatory	Export finance	Extends loan facilities to finance export trade.

TABLE 11.1 *(continued)*

Name of Institution	Type of Institution	Type of Scheme	Main Content of Scheme
Amex International Inc. of USA (on USAID contract in Ghana)	Facilitatory	Technical assistance	Provides technical assistance services to nontraditional export firms (e.g., market identification, market analysis, upgrading of production and management capacity)
Signa One	Facilitatory	Policy guidelines	Assists MOTI in making the policy framework export friendly.
Medium-Term Plan for Nontraditional Exports (MTP-NTE)	Facilitatory	Sector development services	Diversification of the export base and increasing nontraditional exports' share of total exports.
Private Enterprise Foundation (PEF)	Facilitatory	Coordination	Sustains dialogue between the government and the private sectors.
Ghana Standards Board (GSB)	Facilitatory	Quality standards	Ensure quality standards to make exports competitive.
Ghana Trade Fairs Authority	Promotional/ facilitatory	Exhibition	Organizing local and international trade fairs and exhibitions

Source: Adapted from Tetteh, 1996, p. 65.

Another relevant public institution is the Bank of Ghana, which handles and regulates all foreign currency transactions. In addition, some exporting firms have to seek approval from specific ministries and public institutions for their export activities. These include the Ministry of Food and Agriculture, for food exporters; Forest Inspection Bureau, for the export of wood products; or the Museums and Monuments Board, for the export of handicrafts. These and similar institutions play regulatory roles within the export business sector.

Judging from the list of institutions and the nature of their activities, it is apparent that the government has set out to establish an elaborate institutional framework with a view toward effectively supporting the development of the export sector. The issue addressed in the rest of this chapter is the images that these institutions have carved within the export business sector: Are their activities geared to the needs of the firms? Are the firms aware of the various facilities that they offer? To what extent do they use them? How do the firms perceive the institutional context in general? These questions are addressed for each of the three categories of institutions listed previously.

PROMOTIONAL INSTITUTIONS

The role of export promotion in the development of a viable export sector has been repeatedly stressed in the literature. Firms of all sizes, in both developed and the developing countries, require some direct support to initiate their export activities. The general understanding is that export promotion services will have the greatest beneficial effect if targeted at firms in their early stages of internationalization (Seringhaus and Botschen, 1991) because export activities produce lower levels of profit than domestic business (Kotabe and Czinkota, 1992). Even firms that do not have a substantial domestic market to fall back on may be deterred from entering foreign markets by the high degree of uncertainty that characterizes export business. Export promotion schemes are put in place to lower managers' perceived and actual risks in connection with their export activities, thereby easing the decision-making process.

Of the promotional and facilitatory agencies presented in Table 11.1, only the Ghana Export Promotion Council (GEPC) appears, thus far, to have made a distinctive impact on the operations of the firms. The GEPC was established in 1969 and operates under the aegis of the Ministry of Trade and Industries. It is specifically responsible for the development of a diversified export base for the economy through the creation of export awareness within the business community and the provision of the skills and services necessary to optimally utilize the country's nontraditional export potential.

The following three activities of the GEPC have received the most attention and favorable ratings:

1. *Fairs and exhibitions.* The GEPC works closely with the Trade Fairs Authority to arrange trade fairs and exhibitions in Ghana in which potential importers participate. In addition, it informs registered exporters about fairs in potentially attractive foreign

markets and encourages them to attend. For most of the small and newly established firms, these arrangements provide them with the only real opportunity to meet potential importers. As indicated in Table 10.1, 35 percent of the firms obtained their first orders through participation in GEPC-sponsored fairs.

2. *Market information and new market leads.* Being the best-organized promotional institution in the country, the GEPC is in contact with leading trade organizations in potential export markets as well as such multilateral agencies as the United Nations-financed International Trade Center (ITC). Through these links, GEPC is able to provide Ghanaian exporters with useful market information to assist them in their market selection decisions. GEPC is also the first stop for foreign trading firms or their agencies interested in sourcing their goods from Ghana. Their enquiries at GEPC are then passed on to local exporters dealing in products of interest to the enquirers. Of the firms in this study, 25 percent received enquiries from prospective importers through the GEPC.

3. *Export awards.* In addition to these services, GEPC has instituted an annual award program in recognition of extraordinary export performance, with are various categories of awards. The highest award, the gold medal, includes a cash prize of US$2,500 to be used on a business trip to the country of the winner's choice. The gold medal goes to the firm with the highest export sales in a given year (but not less than US$500,000). Firms within specified product categories compete for the awards each year.

About 80 percent of the firms covered in this study have been award winners, some on three consecutive occasions. The gold medals are usually conspicuously displayed in the chief executive's office as a mark of distinction and a symbol of company pride. The motivational value of these awards should not be underestimated.

Apart from the GEPC, the Ghana Investment Promotion Centre (GIPC) has also received some credit, but just from a few firms that have obtained tax exemptions for machines and equipment they imported. For the majority of the exporting firms with a minimum of equipment in use, these facilities are of marginal or no relevance.

The Ghana National Chamber of Commerce (GNCC) and the Trade Promotion Unit (TPU) of the Ministry of Trade and Industry (MOTI) appear not to have a noticeable promotional impact on the firms interviewed.

FACILITATORY INSTITUTIONS

The overall assessment is that the government-established facilitatory institutions play a less significant role than is expected by the exporting firms. The foreign-sponsored agencies appear to be doing better than the local ones. The United States Agency for International Development (USAID)-sponsored Trade and Investment Program (TIP) has been mentioned by 20 percent of the respondents as making notable contributions to the export business environment. One firm gave TIP credit for the abolition of the *export proceeds retention scheme,* which required exporters to deposit with banks 65 percent of their proceeds free of interest. The idea underlying the establishment of the Export Finance Company (EFC) was considered laudable, but the operations and procedures of the company have been found to be too sluggish to be relied upon.

The Federation of Association of Ghanaian Exporters (FAGE) and the product associations, on the other hand, stand prominently in the minds of respondents as making substantial contributions to the development of the export sector. Since the members of these associations are exporters themselves, the activities engaged in by the associations are directly aimed at removing operational bottlenecks and promoting sustainable growth. The Kola Nut Exporters Association, for example, has been instrumental in reopening the Togo-Ghana border for kola nut traffic after its closure for political reasons. The association has also supported the development of new hybrids of kola nuts in cooperation with the Cocoa Research Station. The Furniture Producers and Exporters Association has made similar contributions to its members' development.

The rest of the facilitatory institutions are either unknown to the respondents or their activities are believed to have no notable effect on their operations.

REGULATORY INSTITUTIONS

The role of the regulatory institutions is mixed, partly due to the new export incentive programs they have been required to administer in recent years. The Customs, Excise, and Preventive Services (CEPS) is frequently referred to as an institution with potential benefit. This is apparently due to the duty drawback scheme that CEPS administers. The duty drawback scheme works as follows: A firm imports materials and equipment used in producing goods for export. The firm initially pays duties on all the items it imports into the country, as required by the general rules on imports. Once the products (or parts thereof) are exported, however, the firm can apply for a reimbursement of the duties previously paid for the materials that were used in making the export products. The underlying logic of the scheme is fair enough, but many exporters view the procedure for reclaiming duties as unduly cumbersome and time-consuming. Only a small number of firms make the attempt. For firms relying heavily on imported inputs, this represents a lost opportunity to improve their competitive strategies.

The various ministries have a very bad image among exporters. They have been accused of sluggishness, nonprofessionalism, and occasionally for having incomplete knowledge of their areas of administration. This situation creates an atmosphere of conflict rather than collaboration between the exporters and representatives of the public institutions.

On a more positive note, the Ghana Standards Board (GSB) has won the respect of many exporting firms for acting as a guarantor of the quality of their products. As long as GSB's certificate is recognized in the importing countries as evidence of quality, the role of GSB in Ghana's export development should not be underestimated.

In summary, the evidence in this study suggests that only a few institutions clearly stand out as making positive contributions to the export efforts in Ghana. The services of many of the facilitatory agencies appear not to be targeted at the leading exporting firms. It is difficult to say whether the agencies have adopted a deliberate strategy of ignoring the leading firms to concentrate their efforts on the relatively weaker ones. If this is the case, their strategy makes sense. But if the less successful firms feel equally neglected, one can argue that the agencies have yet to find a good working strategy.

Seen in terms of the Partnership Model of relations between government institutions and business organizations, it can be argued that Ghana still has far to go before proper dialogue and cooperation can take place within common institutions. As noted earlier, economic liberalization and the government's pursuit of vigorous policies aimed at promoting private entrepreneurship started only in the mid-1980s. The government may no longer be hostile to private entrepreneurs, but the parties are still suspicious of each other's motives and commitment.

In spite of the current weakness of both public and private institutions and the limited degree of constructive dialogue between them, the Partnership Model of government-business interaction introduced in Chapter 5 does provide an appropriate framework for analyzing the context of international business development in Ghana.

PERCEIVED PROBLEMS AND COPING STRATEGIES IN EXPORT BUSINESS

As shown in Table 11.2, high interest rates and bank charges were mentioned by 70 percent of the respondents as a serious external barrier to the growth of their businesses. Bank credits to exporting firms were estimated at only 4.4 percent of total bank credit in Ghana in 1990 (Baah-Nuakoh et al., 1996). The effective interest rate in the country in 1997 was about 43 percent (ISSER, 1998). Despite the establishment of the Export Finance Company in 1992 to alleviate the financial problems of the exporters, the operations of many exporters are still hamstrung by capital shortages. Although no recent estimates of the ratio of export bank credit to total bank credit are available, informed opinion puts the ratio at the 1990 level.

Apart from financial constraints, the instability of the local currency was mentioned as a serious barrier. The average interbank exchange rate in Ghana has declined steadily over the past fourteen years since the initiation of the structural adjustment program. Recent years have witnessed even more drastic declines. In 1993, the exchange rate between the cedi (the local currency) and the U.S. dollar was 649. It then

TABLE 11.2. Firms' Perceptions of the Seriousness of Export Barriers

Barriers	Major	Minor	None	Total
External Barriers				
High interest rates/bank charges	14	2	4	20
Export procedures/bureaucracy	2	10	8	20
Inadequate infrastructure/ transportation	7	7	6	20
Currency instability	14	—	6	20
Delays in receiving export proceeds	4	3	13	20
Inadequate market information	5	10	5	20
Internal Barriers				
Capital/financing	12	8	—	20
Inadequate supply	8	8	4	20
Inadequate skilled labor	2	6	12	20

Note: Figures represent the number of firms perceiving barriers in each category.

fell to 1,200 cedis to the dollar in 1995 and then to 2,050 cedis to the dollar in 1997 (ISSER, 1998). As previously noted, this decline in the value of the local currency was a primary motivation for many firms' decisions to embark on export business. But where exports are sporadic and firms cannot accumulate substantial foreign currency to finance their imported inputs, the high cedi costs of these inputs become a constraint. The inflationary effect of the declining cedi value on the entire economy also has adversely impacted on the export sector in that it raises the overall costs of operation, thereby eroding the price competitiveness of the firms.

Contrary to the evidence presented in Baah-Nuakoh and colleagues' (1996) study, the bureaucratic institutions do not appear to place any serious constraint on the operations of the firms in the present study. Only two firms see the slow export procedures as a problem, and only three viewed delay in payment of export proceeds with serious concern. Two factors account for this perception. First, there is an increasing awareness within the business community of the present government's commitment to the development of the export sector of the economy. This commitment has been demonstrated partly in the continued efforts made to reform the government institutions with which the exporting firms interact. Second, most managers have developed workable solutions to the most recurrent problems experienced in their contacts with the bureaucracy, and this has become part of the overall Ghanaian business culture.

Market information is also not considered a serious problem. Successful Ghanaian exporting firms emphasize market knowledge acquisition through face-to-face contact with importers and distributors, in conformity with the accepted perception in the export marketing literature (Wiedersheim-Paul, Olson, and Welch, 1978; Schlegelmilch, 1986; McAuley, 1993). This implies that Ghanaian exporters are more inclined to adopt an experiential approach to market knowledge acquisition than to collect objective information through market surveys (cf Eriksson et al., 1997).

In addition to lack of capital, several firms indicated that inadequate supply of inputs is a major constraint to them. The supply problem epitomizes the weak production base of the economy as a whole. Not only are the production bases of the exporting firms small, they cannot rely on a regular supply of raw materials and inputs from other producers. As noted earlier, the firms take their contractual obligations seriously; disruptions caused by delayed and irregular supplies of inputs render them unreliable suppliers in their relationships with importers/distributors.

SUMMARY

The commitment of the present government to export sector development and the establishment of a wide range of promotional institutions have doubtlessly created a stimulating climate for export business. The main difficulty at this stage of the firms' export involvement is the inadequacy of funding, both from internal sources and from established financial institutions. Since this study is focused on the leading exporters, it would be erroneous, however, to assume that all exporting firms in Ghana are capable of overcoming all the other barriers in export business normally faced by new firms. The probability that neophyte exporters will face problems in areas of documentation and bureaucratic procedures should not be ignored. Again, although the firms covered in this study do not consider objective market information as critical to their decisions at the present stage, the situation may be different for nonexporters.

Furthermore, in spite of the establishment of many export promotional and facilitatory institutions in the country, most of the respondents have shown low levels of awareness of their existence and the nature of the services they offer. Previous studies have made similar observations (Katsikeas and Morgan, 1994). The present study has not systematically investigated the reasons for the low awareness level of the respondents with regard to the institutions. A plausible explanation may be that too many of the institutions were established within too short a time, making it difficult for their potential clients to investigate them and determine the differences in their services.

PART III:
REASSESSMENT
OF INTERNATIONALIZATION
THEORIES

The preceding discussions showed that contemporary theories of internationalization are of limited relevance in explaining and guiding the internationalization process of Ghanaian firms and by extension, firms in other developing countries. We can now reexamine the theories and consider alternative schemes of conceptualization and analysis of the internationalization process of developing country firms that share backgrounds and profiles similar to those covered in this study. The analytical scheme we propose is informed by three key arguments:

1. The plurality and contextual embeddedness of business systems found in the world economy today. The argument is that the world now contains a diversity of successful patterns of business development so strategic opportunities of firms cannot be adequately assessed without an insight into their operational context.
2. The multiplicity of approaches to internationalization available to developing country-based firms due to global competition and the attendant intensification of market and supplier searches by firms in mature market economies.
3. Pressures on governments in developing countries to open up their economies to world trade and foreign investments and to

establish enabling institutional frameworks for the internationalization of their own firms.

These arguments are supported by the empirical evidence from Ghana and are discussed more elaborately in Chapter 12. In Chapter 13,
we recapitulate the highlights of the discussion and draw attention to
some research implications of the study.

Chapter 12

The Context and Approaches to the Internationalization of Firms in Developing Countries

Recent literature on comparative business studies indicates a drift in consensus from the notion of the universality of business development theories to the recognition of a wide variety of successful business development "recipes" throughout the world. It is now recognized that institutional structures, such as political systems of authority and coordination, patterns of dependence, and the foundations of social identities, combine with physical infrastructural systems to shape the pattern of business development in every country (Hamilton and Biggart, 1988; Whitley, 1992, 1994).

Arguably, therefore, each country can develop a unique enterprise structure and practices that can function as successfully as those found in Western industrialized economies. This provides both opportunities and challenges for cross-national interfirm relations. The opportunities arise from the unique competencies and advantages that firms in every country can develop on the basis of the particulars of their organizing context. Cross-national interfirm relations can therefore produce mutually reinforcing synergies that may raise the competitive positions of the collaborating partners. The challenge derives from the awareness that contextual differences can create communication difficulties during the initial stages of interfirm relations, thereby weakening the basis of trust necessary for building an enduring relationship.

The empirical evidence and theories discussed in the preceding chapters gain additional meaning when considered against the background of these observations. The essential point is that to understand the approaches, processes, and patterns of internationalization of firms in any given country, one needs to examine the context within which they operate. This is the task examined in the rest of this chapter. We first provide an overview of the operational context of Ghanaian firms to serve as an illustration of the relevance of context to business development in a developing country. We then introduce two broad internationalization approaches—downstream versus upstream internationalization—and discuss factors influencing managers' choice of either or both of the approaches. The final discussion focuses on the importance of institutional changes taking place in some developing countries (including Ghana) to guide and support the process of internationalization and their implications for the competitive performance of these firms.

CONTEXT OF BUSINESS DEVELOPMENT AND INTERNATIONALIZATION

An understanding of the current context of private entrepreneurship; export business development in Ghana, in particular; and developing economies, in general, requires an awareness of the features and consequences of postindependence government economic policies as well as the sociocultural frame of entrepreneurial activities. As indicated in Chapter 7, the first thirty years of Ghana's postindependence economic history (1957-1984) were characterized by a remarkable consistency in successive governments' distrust for private entrepreneurship. State ownership and/or control of business activities was the hallmark of the country's economic development policy during this period, which was been characterized by drastic decline in all aspects of the economy due to a combination of internal economic mismanagement and negative external economic environment. Since 1984, the country has embarked on a World Bank cum International Monetary Fund (IMF)-sponsored structural adjustment program aimed at economic rehabilitation and growth. This program includes a reversal of the economic policies of the previous governments in favor of private enterprise development and an opening up of the economy to foreign goods and investors (ISSER, 1997).

The export strategies of the companies covered in this study were motivated by this change in economic policy. Ghana's economy, in general, has again begun to grow, but at a considerably slow pace when compared to Asian economies. Ghanaian companies have not yet demonstrated any distinctive competitive advantages in the international market. In addition, the change in the government's overall economic policy has not yet produced the required changes in the mind-set of public institutions. That is, the relationship between the business community and the public institutions is still noncollaborative and, on occasion, confrontational. It is fair to argue that both the government and the business community are still in the process of building new collaborative arrangements and modus operandi.

As the empirical results indicate, the emerging private entrepreneurial group in Ghana still lacks a solid capital base, and many business owners are engaged in fragmentary business activities. The decision to operate a diversified portfolio of investments is meant to serve as a strategic hedge against uncertainties inherent in an exporting operational context and to accommodate certain sociocultural demands, such as finding jobs for unemployed members of one's extended family.

With respect to the sociocultural aspects of the business context in Ghana, it can be noted that the extended family's patterns of dependence on the local entrepreneurs affect recruitment and other personnel policies in the firms, a situation foreign companies may find unacceptable. Furthermore, the less vibrant organizational climate and autocratic management styles found in Ghanaian firms reduce the staff's ability to be innovative and to learn quickly from their foreign partners. On a positive note, the growing nonkin trust relations within the Ghanaian business community (i.e., social networks established in alumni and old boys associations) provide the local businessperson with a good opportunity to gain access to resources within the Ghanaian economy (Sørensen and Kuada, 1997).

The characteristics of the business context outlined here are not peculiar to Ghana. The economies of most African countries south of the Sahara have been victims of similar experiments with state entrepreneurship, undisciplined implementation of economic policies, combined with unfavorable trends in external trade. These factors have jointly produced a drastic economic decline of a magnitude similar to the one found in Ghana. The sociocultural context within which businesses in these other African countries operate is remarkably similar to that of Ghana (see Leonard, 1987; Montgomery, 1987; and Kuada, 1994, for elaboration).

However, before becoming overwhelmed by the many intercultural problems, it must be remembered that entrepreneurs are not captives of their cultural context. Although the macrocultures of their ambient societies provide them with the organizing context of their activities, entrepreneurs are both perceptive to and receptive of signals and opportunities that lie outside this immediate context, constantly seeing themselves in different roles and situations. Put differently, the entrepreneur undertakes personal interpretations of the cultural context in which he or she operates, and this shapes the "reality" underlying his or her business decisions.

The empirical results reported in this study provide clear support for this perception. The leading Ghanaian exporting firms, such as Combined Farmers, Astek Limited, Getrade, and Kiku Company Limited, do not succumb entirely to the obligations that the Ghanaian culture imposes on successful businesspeople. They actually adopt strategies that mitigate perceived negative cultural effects on their businesses without jeopardizing their culturally ascribed status. This is demonstrated clearly in their recruitment policies. Each of the aforementioned companies has discouraged employment of distant relatives in their businesses to avoid its negative impact on the motivation of other employees. The companies have also evolved effective means of avoiding the bureaucratic constraints inherent in Ghanaian public institutions. At the same time, they have been able to use their established networks not for rent seeking but for genuine productive activities. These observations about the context of business development in Ghana have prompted us to explore the various approaches that developing country firms can adopt to internationalize their businesses.

Another important consideration in the study of the internationalization process of developing country firms is the wide variety of foreign market entry modes available to them. As discussed in Chapters 5 and 6, alliances with other local companies (to develop and export new products) as well as outsourcing arrangements of foreign firms are among the strategic options that developing country firms can consider. Strategic alliances also enhance firms' ability to improve their competitive positions within the global market.

The policies of most governments in developing countries during the past two decades have contributed immensely to the feasibility of cross-national collaborations between firms. As noted in the case of Ghana (see Chapter 7), the structural adjustment program initiated in 1984 has specifically aimed at liberalizing the domestic market. All key sectors, including banking, telecommunication, manufacturing, and agriculture, have been opened to private local and foreign investors. Similar programs have been implemented in a number of other African countries with varying degrees of success (Kuada and Sørensen, 1995). Furthermore, as discussed in Chapter 5, many developing countries have designed incentive packages to attract foreign investors into their countries. All these policy initiatives impact on the internationalization process of firms in the developing countries.

APPROACHES TO THE INTERNATIONALIZATION OF FIRMS IN DEVELOPING COUNTRIES

To explore the internationalization modes, the revealed diversity has been encapsulated into two main approaches to the integration of developing country-based firms into the world economy:

1. Internationalization through *downstream activities*
2. Internationalization through *upstream activities*

Whereas internationalization through downstream activities represents the conventional approach to the study of internationalization, internationalization through upstream activities appears to be the more likely route of integrating developing country companies into the world economy, given the context within which their internationalization takes place.

Arguably, developing country firms may initiate their internationalization process using an upstream approach—i.e., without engaging in conventional downstream activities. In an extreme case, a firm may be acquired by a global company and hence become a single unit in a coordinated global network of units and activities. Or it may enter into a strategic alliance with a foreign company that provides it with technical and managerial know-how, enabling it to become more competitive on the domestic market.

Each of the two basic approaches to the integration of the company into the world economy can be divided into three subapproaches, as shown in Figure 12.1.

Downstream Integration into the World Economy

Downstream integration represents the conventional view of internationalization that focuses attention exclusively on the marketing of finished goods and services in a foreign country, especially through exports. As shown in Figure 12.1, developing country firms may enter foreign markets through their own export initiatives or by acting as a regular supplier to an outsourcing company from a mature market economy. These options are discussed in greater detail in the following material.

FIGURE 12.1. Approaches to the Internationalization and Integration of Developing Country-Based Firms into the Global Economy

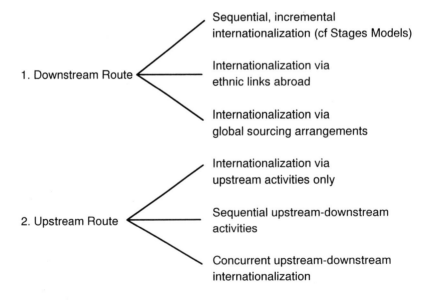

Internationalization According to the Stages Models

Proposition 1:

Based on local resources and free access to neighboring countries, companies in developing countries will start exporting according to the Stages Models of internationalization.

As discussed previously, the Stages Models hold that firms use their own resources to create competitive market advantages for their products abroad. Furthermore, since firms have little or no international experience prior to their first export orders, the internationalization is organized as an incremental learning experience process. The commitment to internationalization increases gradually.

The Stages Models assume that international activities start by entering nearby culturally similar countries. Ghanaian companies, similar to companies in other African countries, can only follow the prescriptions of the Stages Models if the following conditions are met: First, the overwhelming orientation of the companies toward the former colonial powers and mature market economies, in general, rather than toward neighboring countries must cease. Second, the institutional barriers that impede intra-African trade, i.e., exports and imports between neighboring countries, must be reduced. Third, the companies must adopt strategies that ensure an increase in the added value of their products. For example, the same basic foodstuffs and raw materials are produced within the West African subregion; Ghanaian companies create differential advantages only through processing these items to increase the added value that they offer their customers in the subregion.

It should be noted, however, that unofficial exports and imports between Ghana and neighboring countries have always taken place. At times, when the currency policies in neighboring countries were not in harmony, this trade could be rather comprehensive. With reference to the present trend in developing countries toward the formation of regional customs unions and free trading areas, it can be expected that companies and traders will start exporting to neighboring countries in a pattern similar to the one indicated by the Stages Models.

There is, however, some evidence indicating that Ghanaian companies export unprocessed foodstuffs (e.g., maize) to countries in the Sahel subzone due to their locational comparative advantages (Ghana being located in the forest belt). Various manufactured goods, such as aluminium kitchen utensils and plastic items are also exported to neighboring countries such as Togo and Côte d'Ivoire, presumably because Ghanaian companies have competitive advantages in the production and marketing of these items.

Internationalization Through Ethnic Links

Proposition 2:

Companies in developing countries can overcome problems of cultural dissonance by exporting through ethnic links abroad.

As shown in Chapter 9, some Ghanaian exports are targeted at Ghanaian (and other African) residents abroad. They are sold mainly through distribution channels that are organized and managed by Ghanaians. Exporting through ethnic linkages is thus a viable alternative that is not restricted to products aimed at Ghanaians; it can be used to export any type of goods for the general market, granting the Ghanaian managed channels are competitive and effective compared with alternative channels.[1]

The possibility of ethnic channel systems tends to overcome a key barrier assumed in the Stages Models, i.e., the cultural differences between the exporter and the foreign channel members. Selling through channel members with the same cultural background as the exporter reduces the incidence of communication errors and suspicion. Interchannel cooperation is likely to be closer, and the effectiveness of marketing efforts will be enhanced.

However, a few cases indicate that the assumed trust in interethnic business relations is not always present. That is, Ghanaian businesspeople distrust their fellow Ghanaians abroad and, therefore will supervise them closely. This thesis of ethnic distrust needs to be further investigated.

Internationalization by Global Industry/Company Inducement

Proposition 3:

The international sourcing of local resource-based products and labor-intensive manufactures by companies in mature market economies has reduced the need for firms in developing countries to engage in elaborate market search activities to become integrated into the world economy.

The downstream internationalization process of companies based in the developing countries may be triggered by sourcing activities of global companies located in mature market economies. Normally, internationalization is measured in terms of a company's export volume. However, import volumes can provide a good indication of the degree of internationalization of companies that sell their products largely on the domestic market. In other words, many companies are very proactive and source globally. In fact, global sourcing has become one of the most important methods by which global companies sustain their competitive advantage.

These companies, which are located primarily in the mature market economies, use two modes of global sourcing:

1. Procurement of inputs and final products
2. Subcontracting or production contracts

In the first case, a company in the developing country may become a principal supplier of inputs to production enterprises or of final products to chain stores in the market economies. The major products Ghana is capable of supplying to these categories of customers are, at present, cocoa products and pineapples. In the second case of production contracts, the developing country-based company produces according to designs and other instructions provided by the buyer from the mature market economy; the latter may even supply the essential inputs used in the production process. A developing country-based company may be fortuitously discovered by an outsourcer located in the developed country, or it may make itself known to the outsourcer through specific marketing initiatives. In the former case, the company may passively wait for an unsolicited visit by a global company, perhaps not even realizing that its products have international market potential. In the latter case, the company may register with, for example, a local export promotion council, as foreign sourcing companies often contact various institutions to acquire lists of potential producers. Along the same line, a would-be exporter in the developing country may search for global customers through embassies, business colleagues, friends, business associations, as well as other institutions through which a global sourcer may be reached. Our empirical evidence indicated that Ghanaian firms look for foreign importers mainly by attending local and overseas exhibitions or looking them up in trade directories.

Such induced internationalization is not without problems and risks. First of all, local companies that adopt this approach gain relatively little international experience because the global sourcer takes care of everything. Our data indicate that, in several cases, Ghanaian managers have not even had the opportunity to pay visits to their customers in the importing countries. Second, the global sourcing company may look for static efficiency and not dynamic efficiency. As such, it may shift sources of supply if companies from any other country come up with competitively superior packages. Third, the risk of opportunistic behavior on the part of the sourcer is high.

Upstream Approaches to Internationalization

As argued previously, the general assumption in the existing literature is that internationalization is a *downstream* activity, i.e., selling or producing products (or modifications thereof) to buyers in other countries. This, by implication, means that firms who sell their products exclusively on the domestic market are not viewed in the literature as being international, although they might be actively engaged in transactions with foreign companies (e.g., sourcing inputs and other resources abroad). We argue that this limited perception of the concept of internationalization restricts the scope of analysis and range of strategic options available to firms in the developing countries. In this section, we present and discuss the concept of *upstream internationalization* and variations thereof as an alternative approach to the conventional perspective on internationalization. The concept upstream internationalization, as used here, covers all forms of transactions and relationships in which a manufacturing firm in a developing country engages with foreign firms to strengthen its operational capacities, i.e., a focus on the input side of the value-added chain.

As will become evident from the following discussions, upstream and downstream internationalization are not mutually exclusive approaches in the internationalization processes of firms. Rather, they serve different and very often complementary purposes. The two types of international activity can therefore operate concurrently or sequentially, and one type of activity may be more dominant at certain periods in the history of the firm than the other. Thus, the following variants of upstream internationalization can be identified:

1. Internationalization by upstream activities only
2. Sequential upstream-downstream internationalization
3. Concurrent upstream-downstream internationalization

The upstream activities play a critical role in defining the overall strategies as well as the tempo and direction of firms' internationalization process. The decision of firms to base their internationalization process on upstream activities, however, will depend on their overall motives behind internationalization and their prospects of finding suitable partners abroad. These observations have guided the propositions and discussions that follow.

Internationalization by Upstream Activities Only

Proposition 4:

Growth-oriented manufacturing firms in developing countries can raise their capacities to compete at home by engaging in upstream international activities.

This proposition reflects the context within which developing country businesses are organized. It is generally acknowledged that manufacturing firms in the developing countries face low and/or stagnating domestic demand for their products, soaring relative prices for their inputs and equipment, as well as low technological capabilities (Lall and Wignaraja, 1996). In several African countries, the demand constraints have been aggravated by the declining levels of income of certain sections of the community due to the impact of structural adjustment programs (SAPs) being undertaken. At the same time, the trade liberalization components of SAPs have engendered intensive competition with relatively more competent foreign manufacturers. The combination of these factors makes it strategically imperative for local firms to strengthen their competitive positions both at home and abroad. As the empirical evidence indicated, firms having locally induced unique competence (e.g., uniquely designed products) have fairly good opportunities to sell their products at a premium to relatively small market segments abroad, thereby raising the capacity utilization of their equipment and resources.

The competitive capacities of most of these firms, however, are severely constrained by the low level of their technological capabilities and managerial competence. This reduces the comparative advantages that firms in these countries are expected to enjoy in producing labor-intensive products such as garments or local resource-based products such as furniture.

Upgrading the technological capability of a firm and industry is, however, a costly and time-consuming process involving unlearning old habits and replacing them with new ones. For this reason, Lall and Wignaraja (1996) argue against unrestricted import liberalization and in favor of state interventions that restrict imports of products whose production is based on complex technological capabilities. The economic history of developing countries, however, has eloquently shown how inadvisable local industry protection under the "infant industry" umbrella can be. For one thing, the world market scene is not static, and the players therein are continuously raising their own competitive capabilities. It will therefore be foolhardy to insulate developing country firms from these changes. Furthermore, as argued by Lall and Wignaraja, firms constrained by low-level technological capabilities may not even know what their deficiencies are, let alone be able to remedy them on their own. The weak domestic market in itself can hardly provide the firms with the challenges that can trigger a change. This is a classical paradox of growth: protection against unfair competition provides disincentives for local firms to invest, innovate, and grow.

A way to manage this paradox and raise the performance level of firms in developing countries such as Ghana is to encourage them to engage in intensive and long-term relationships with foreign firms to raise their technological and managerial capacities. This approach to firm growth has been captured in recent literature in the concept of strategic alliances.

Firms that are engaged in upstream relations aimed at strengthening their domestic market positions will focus on sourcing quality inputs and equipment from foreign sources with favorable conditions of payment and opportunities for training workers in efficient input usage. Upstream relationships can also be developed with local subsidiaries of international companies that have the capacity to provide the requisite skills and resources. Since African firms are already established in their local markets and networks, the upgrading of their technological capacities can be incremental (i.e., gradual) rather than dramatic. The evolutionary process of the change is less resource demanding (in terms of material investments, managerial time spent on its implementation, and psychological adjustments inherent in the learning process). It also provides them with the opportunity to make the adjustment process acceptable to organization members.

For the foreign firms participating in this arrangement, their transactions with developing country firms will constitute downstream internationalization, i.e., selling equipment, knowledge, and raw materials. Their decisions to participate in such relationships will depend on their assessment of how these relationships fit into their overall international business objectives and strategies.

Sequential Upstream-Downstream Internationalization

Proposition 5:

Developing country-based manufacturing firms with low technological capabilities may initiate their internationalization processes with an upstream approach to raise their subsequent export performance on the global market.

Sequential upstream-downstream internationalization implies that upstream activities and relations precede the initiation of downstream transactions. The former relations, however, are not terminated when downstream internationalization begins. They may, in fact, increase in range and complexity in response to changing needs of the firm.

Downstream internationalization may be deliberately planned to succeed the upstream internationalization process, or it may be unintended but seen as a logical consequence of successful upstream activities. In the first case, firms engaged in the upstream relationship do so intentionally to support their downstream internationalization processes. The strategic goal of the upstream activities, in this regard, is to raise the competitive capacity of the focal developing country firms in their chosen export markets. Therefore, the success of the upstream internationalization is measured by the success of the downstream internationalization. In the second case, the downstream internationalization becomes an emergent rather than a deliberate strategy. For one thing, doing business with international suppliers gives international exposure to a firm's management. Information about market opportunities abroad may be generated through these contacts. Having a position within an international business network as a buyer, management finds it relatively easier to explore opportunities in these markets for its products or as a strategic alliance partner. Thus, market selection flows naturally from these initial contacts.

Where the focal firm aims at being a major player on the international scene, i.e., using upstream internationalization as a springboard for downstream internationalization, an incremental approach to change may not prove effective. The pace of change in this situation will depend on the firm's level of technological capability prior to the upstream internationalization, as well as the degree of international competition in the products and markets in which it intends to operate. Firms with very low levels of technological capability compared to the major players in the target markets may require dramatic changes in their profiles, i.e., in terms of technology, financial resources, technical skill, and managerial competence. To upgrade a company in this case, a strong international strategic alliance or even a joint venture may be needed.

A debatable question is whether developing country firms should engage in upstream relations with a single foreign firm or with several firms. The decision on the number of foreign firms with which to cooperate will depend on the focal firm's internal capacity to coordinate, absorb, and transform varieties of ideas and resources from different foreign partners as well as its ability to honor the obligations that the various relationships impose. Above all, however, the number of foreign firms interested in engaging in relationships with the developing country firm will depend on the latter's comparative attractiveness.

Concurrent Upstream-Downstream Internationalization

Proposition 6:

Developing country manufacturing firms with relatively high technological capabilities operating in supportive macroenvironments stand a better chance of attracting foreign partners for an upstream relationship.

As argued earlier, firms in developing countries are generally not attractive candidates for international firms in search of partners abroad, except for the production of specific product categories for which resource location provides a significant comparative advantage, e.g., wood products and tropical farm products. However, since many developing countries compete with one another on the basis of these advantages, it is fair to argue that the comparative attractiveness of the firms will determine their chances of finding reliable and supportive foreign partners. Comparative attractiveness will depend on

1. the entrepreneurial and human resource profile of the firms, i.e., the level of education and the degree of international exposure of the proprietors or CEOs and other key managers, and
2. the macroenvironment profile of the firms, i.e.,
   - the behavior of the promotional, facilitatory, and regulatory institutions;
   - the general political and economic climate; and
   - the degree of foreign business confidence in the country.

As shown in Lall and Wignaraja's (1996) analysis of the Ghanaian manufacturing sector, several of the leading Ghanaian firms can be assessed as comparatively attractive on the basis of these criteria and, therefore, stand a good chance of attracting foreign firms interested in the African subregion of the global economy.

The critical determinant of enduring interfirm relationships is that they must meet the standard of reciprocity (Wilkins and Ouchi, 1983); i.e., each party gives something of value (e.g., services) and receives something of value (e.g., money). Transaction Costs Theory postulates that the exchange relationship in which firms engage is mediated by economic calculations, as reflected in a price mechanism. Transaction costs, as Ouchi (1980) argues, increase in exchange relationships because the parties involved cannot agree on the real value of what is exchanged or do not trust each other. If transactions underlying the relationship cannot be unequivocally defined in sufficiently detailed contracts to ensure the equitable assessment of value, fear may linger between the parties that self-interested individuals may take undue advantage of the transactions.

Our perspective of strategic alliances between firms in the industrial and developing countries differs from the view expressed in the Transactions Costs Theory. We see these relationships as enduring and evolving rather than motivated by short-term speculations and gains. Underlying such relationships is the belief that, in the long run, all parties involved in the collective effort will be equitably rewarded. The desired outcome, therefore, is long-term goal congruence rather than short-term gains. What binds the parties together is the sharing of general assumptions regarding their cooperation rather than the immediate convergence of specific goals (Wilkins and Ouchi, 1983). The goals and strategies can be described as emergent (rather than fixed) and as evolving through the process of interaction (Sørensen and Kuada, 1998b).

INTERNATIONALIZATION
AND THE INSTITUTIONAL CONTEXT

The general context of firms in developing countries has been outlined previously. This section continues the discussion, focusing on specific contextual issues of importance to the internationalization of companies, such as the following:

1. Industry/product associations
2. Industrial districts
3. Public export and foreign direct investment (FDI) promotion programs

The discussion assumes that the developing country pursues a liberalization and privatization policy, i.e., that the role of the government is basically one of facilitation and promotion rather than regulation and direction of activities.

Industry/Product Associations

Industry associations are organizations established by private companies to promote the interests of the members of the associations. Basically, such associations have two roles:

1. Representing the members vis-à-vis outsiders, e.g., the government and other institutions that influence the work of the industry and the companies
2. Servicing the members, e.g., institutionalizing ethical codes of conduct, encouraging interfirm cooperation and information flow

As evident from the empirical results discussed in Chapter 11, Ghanaian export firms have established a number of industry/product associations to provide them with promotional facilities and to lobby government institutions.

Because Ghana, unlike some Asian countries (Whitley, 1992; Hamilton and Biggart, 1988), has no existing network of trading houses with international experience, industry associations play an important role (together with government promotional institutions, discussed later) in closing the gap between Ghanaian manufacturers and foreign markets. One way of doing this is to develop a strong culture for collective action abroad. By pooling resources, Ghanaian companies may be able to match their stronger competitors abroad. Another way is to serve as mediators for individual companies. This involves not just finding a partner abroad but also developing a complete package that enables the company to get started in the international market.

The associations are also expected to play an important role in ensuring fair play between foreign companies and their members, in both the domestic and foreign markets. However, in their present situation, their capacity to play such a role is limited.

The role of the associations must also be seen in terms of their contribution to the development of other dimensions of the operational context, through their relations with government and through the development of industrial districts.

Industrial Districts

The explorative study presented in this book has not revealed the existence of any genuine industrial district in Ghana. On the contrary, the ongoing debate in the country centers on the creation of "export zones" in an attempt to attract foreign investments. Some indication of incipient industrial districts can be observed, however, within the pineapple and aluminium products industries.

These emerging industrial districts may derive some inspiration from the cut-flower industry in East Africa. For example, cut-flower exports from Kenya were started by a foreign company that designed a strategy for encouraging local cultivation of exportable cut flowers. As local entrepreneurs started entering the industry, the foreign company supported them with technical knowledge. The industry grew rapidly, resulting in shortages of qualified cut-flower workers and managers. Companies within the industry, therefore, found it worthwhile to form an association that could coordinate their activities and improve their resource base.

As argued in Chapter 5, industrial districts can provide a framework for dynamic interaction among firms. Through these interactions, firms can jointly upgrade their skills and technology and stimulate one another to engage in continuous improvement of their core competencies. It is this process of mutual reinforcement that produces dynamic (rather than static) efficiency within firms (Porter, 1994)

One general conclusion deserving reiteration is that the emergence of an industrial district does not result from consciously pursued local or regional industrial strategies. The available evidence suggests a two-stage development: spontaneous growth followed by institutionally enhanced growth. It seems that the institutions play a more important role in the second stage; i.e., the policies are not concerned with the emergence of industrial districts but with the path they take once they come into being (Schmitz and Musyck, 1994).

Following this argument further, it should be noted that a theory of internationalization of companies cannot be restricted to company analysis and market research. The local business context within which the company is embedded is crucial, not so much from the viewpoint of static efficiency, but from the perspective of innovation, entrepreneurship, contacts, etc. The public sector as facilitator of industrial district dynamics is also essential, as detailed in the next section.

Public Export and FDI Promotion Programs

The role of the government is on the agenda in all the market-oriented developing countries. The government's new role has to emerge from a period during which governments were hostile to private entrepreneurs and business. The present atmosphere between the old structures of the public sector and the emerging new private sector is one of suspicion.

Our findings from Ghana show that this move from hostility to suspicion has taken place at the same time as both the private and public sectors are in the process of developing institutions that can overcome some of the barriers facing Ghanaian companies that intend to go international. There are some indications that the institutional setup will gradually remove the suspicion and give way to continuous cooperation and dialogue within a set of semiautonomous and loosely coordinated institutions, each of which will cater to one or more needs of the exporting companies.

This stage has not yet been reached. Although the government has established several export promotion schemes, the agencies that implement the schemes still feel "superior" in their relations with companies. Elsewhere (Sørensen and Kuada, 1997), we have argued that governments must refrain from policies of domination within the business sectors of their countries and must instead adopt a Partnership Model as a framework for managing such relationships. That is, their relationships with the business communities must be characterized by mutual respect and dialog.

The assumptions underlying the Partnership Model of the relationship between the public and private sectors are as follows:

- The relationship is dynamic. It is not possible to decide, once and for all, on the proper role of the state.
- A partnership does not mean that no inherent conflicts exist between the public and private sectors. They do, but a partnership mode of organization is a way to resolve the conflicts.
- A partnership atmosphere is innovative. By discussing common problems, creative new ideas will emerge to solve the problems at hand and new ideas and views will continuously emerge from the dialogue. Although it is generally believed that solving one problem creates numerous other problems, it is equally true that in the process of solving one problem, many new ideas beyond the actual problem may emerge.

The theoretical underpinnings of this Partnership Model were detailed in Chapter 6. What is important to stress is that a theory of internationalization of companies must include an understanding of the regulative and promotional mechanisms adopted by the state.

SUMMARY

In summary, developing country-based firms operate in national business contexts remarkably distinct from their counterparts in the mature market economies. Not only are the companies small and resource deficient, but the domestic markets for their products are relatively weak and infrastructural support services are nonexistent in some cases. Until recently, government attitudes and policies have been hostile toward businesses. For these reasons, firms' abilities to develop core competences and products through their own efforts have been considerably weak. Against this background, the business development response, in general, and the export response, in particular, have been relatively modest. We have drawn a distinction between the classical downstream or export route to internationalization and an upstream route. An upstream route to integration into the global economy appears in many cases to be a necessary first step toward an effective downstream internationalization, as this offers the companies opportunities to enhance their technological and management capacities. To achieve the full benefits of upstream internationalization, a dynamic institutional context needs to be developed. We have stressed the benefits of continuous dialogue between private entrepreneurs and public institutions in a partnership spirit. We have further argued in favor of formalized liaison institutions established to encourage such a dialogue, since this will help the involved parties to focus their attention and energies to find pragmatic solutions to recurrent problems and will inspire them to work toward a mutually endorsed vision. In addition to government-business partnership institutions, we also acknowledge important roles that such industry-based associations as product groups and industrial districts can play in developing an enabling, organizing, and nurturing context for the emergent entrepreneurial activities in the developing economies.

Chapter 13

Exploring the Internationalization Process of Developing Country Firms: Policies, Strategies, and Research Agenda

This study reviewed the contemporary theories and models of internationalization of firms and explored their relevance to firms in developing economies. Three categories of models were discussed: (1) Stages Models, (2) Contingency Models, and (3) (Inter)Action Models. We drew attention to limitations of the specific theories and models and suggested modifications, where possible, to make them as relevant as possible to any investigation of the internationalization process of developing country-based firms. A fundamental weakness of all the theories is that they are based on evidence from firms in Western mature market economies. As such, they are not of universal applicability, i.e., applicable to all firms in all countries. This weakness was revealed in the investigation of the internationalization process of the twenty leading Ghanaian exporting firms reported in Part II.

This chapter recapitulates the book's main arguments for quick reference and to highlight their policy and strategy implications, as well as issues that we consider require urgent research attention.

OVERVIEW OF THE THEORETICAL DISCUSSION

We anticipated in the theoretical review that the Stages Models, which emphasize a gradual, sequential, and learning approach to internationalization, can provide a useful guide to our understanding of the export motives and market choices of developing country firms that choose to start their internationalization process in neighboring markets. The models will be of limited relevance, however, for firms that decide to initiate their internationalization processes by selling to customers in distant mature market economies. This observation led us to examine whether the Ghanaian firms choose their neighboring West African countries as their first markets of entry or prefer the more distant European and North American markets. We also argued that the Stages Models' assumption of gradual experiential market knowledge acquisition may apply to many of the companies in the developing countries.

The rationale and assumptions underlying the Contigency Models tend to fit developing country situations. However, the theories often assume comprehensive analyses that go beyond the capacity and relevance of the companies. Furthermore, the guidelines contained in the specific theories (such as the Transaction Costs Theory) are of limited validity since they require the prospective firms to undertake significant investments in the markets of their choice. Considering the limited resources with which firms such as those in Ghana operate, such investments are naturally outside their capacities.

With regard to the relevance of the (Inter)Action Models (e.g., the Network Theory), we expected developing country firms to rely greatly on their existing relationships to find customers abroad. For example, friends, family members, and expatriates may provide important market links to neophyte exporters in these countries because such relationships would minimize the financial resources needed for market and distributor searches. Relying on these links therefore reduces the disadvantages firms incur by virtue of their "latecomer" position in the mature markets. Furthermore, the increasing propensity of chain stores and manufacturers in the mature markets to source their goods, raw materials, and components globally means that some developing country firms could enter these markets without performing any direct market research, except being visible when the global companies come around.

The preliminary theoretical discussions also led us to argue that partnership arrangements in the form of international strategic alliances and collective support through industrial districts could help firms reduce their resource investment requirements and strengthen their technological capacities. However, these arrangements can only succeed within a collaborative government-business relationship.

HIGHLIGHTS OF THE EMPIRICAL RESULTS

Export Motives

It became evident from our empirical investigation that a variety of motives trigger the initial decision of developing country firms to embark on export activities. Some of these motives have been captured in the existing literature on the internationalization processes of firms based in the developed countries. However, some are unique to developing country situations. For example, Ghanaian firms gave the acquisition of foreign currency (to finance imported technology and inputs as well as to pay for other business-related expenditures abroad) as a key motive for embarking on exports. Developing countries facing perennial foreign currency shortages may do well to promote exports if they allow exporters to retain substantial portions of the foreign exchange earnings to finance imports.

Management expectations and faith in export business have also emerged as key internal motives, thereby corroborating the conclusions from previous studies. However, contrary to the view that exporting firms are well nurtured in their domestic markets prior to embarking on export activities, this study showed that many of the exporting firms in developing countries may not have domestic market experience at all. They may be established by an entrepreneur who sees export as a viable business opportunity. Government export policies and schemes may provide the initial triggering cue, directing the entrepreneurs' attention toward the opportunities for selling some of the local products abroad. The entrepreneurs nonetheless enter into the export business with management and business experience from elsewhere. This provides them with a good background to overcome some of the many constraints faced by new exporters.

Export Markets

Contrary to the expectations in the Stages Models, the Ghanaian exporting firms sell to importers/distributors in distant markets of Western Europe and North America because the market potentials in these countries are relatively better for most export products than markets in the nearby countries. Thus, the relative distance of the exporting firms from the final markets for their products, their inexperience, and their small sizes can constitute constraints to their performance in export markets (cf Lall, 1991). Products exported to these markets include tropical fruits and vegetables as well as utilitarian handicrafts, artwork, special wood products, and locally designed garments. Since Ghana has a competitive advantage in the production of many of these products, exporters are able to enter these markets despite the constraints. Subsequent market expansion, however, will require policy intervention that helps the firms overcome these constraints.

Two observations were made regarding accessibility of nearby markets to developing country exporters. The first relates to the distinct differences between the domestic and cross-border markets. It has been assumed in the Stages Models that nearby markets are culturally similar to the domestic markets in terms of business practices. However, due to the historical legacy of developing countries (i.e., their colonial past), the business practices of the various countries are modeled on practices found in different European countries. Thus, the cultural divide between the major European markets is replicated in the developing countries. Cross-border trade can therefore be more problematic in developing countries than usually anticipated in the available literature. The second observation relates to the composition of goods exported to the neighboring countries. In the case of Ghana, most of the cross-border exports consist of light manufactured products such as packaging, plastic products, as well as aluminium sheets and pots. The question is whether the shorter geographical distance that characterizes the cross-border trade can compensate for the technological and experiential advantages of developed country firms that export similar products to the developing countries. Granting limited trade barriers, one can argue that the low labor costs in the developing countries provide them with a competitive edge in the production of standardized, nonbranded products sold to customers in neighboring countries. However, serious visible and invisible barriers that can erode such advantages still exist.

Acquisition of foreign market knowledge by developing country firms proceeds along the same pattern as in the developed countries.

There is a limited use of conventional market surveys and a greater reliance on experimental learning and information obtained through business networks. Nonexporters are encouraged to initiate export activities by friends and business associates, and existing exporters tend to expand their activities to other markets by following market leads obtained through these business networks. A major weakness in this approach to market knowledge acquisition is the low intensity of interaction with overseas importers/distributors. Where the volume of exports is low and deliveries are infrequent, the sporadic interaction with the overseas market actors produces little market experience (Eriksson et al., 1997). That many of the exporters sell to few customers in one or two countries further limits the extent of the foreign market knowledge acquired.

Entry Modes

The findings of this study further indicated that national export promotion strategies in developing countries may encourage the establishment of small export companies managed by their owners. The establishment of such local intermediaries means that many local producers may inadvertently enter into international business by using an indirect mode of export. There will also exist a group of producer-exporters who adopt direct modes of entry. Both local exporting companies and producer-exporters sell to overseas importer-distributors. However, as indicated earlier, the small volumes of their exports, their relatively small sizes, and their inexperience place them in a weak bargaining position in their interactions with foreign buyers. The latter may take advantage of the vulnerability of the developing country exporters by insisting on lower prices for their products and offering them shorter contract periods than is normal within the industry. Relationships with overseas buyers are therefore another area of constraint that export promotion policies must seek to address.

Constraints

The available literature provides a long list of constraints to export business activities. Among them are poor knowledge of export procedures, inadequate managerial skills, delays in receiving export proceeds, low technological capacity, and undercapitalization of the businesses. Most of these constraints affect export businesses in developing countries, but their magnitude will vary according to country, industry, and the operational history of individual firms. The findings from the empirical study in Ghana suggest that undercapitalization and low volumes of local production are among the most serious constraints to the operation of relatively young exporting firms. The banks, thus far, have failed to act as export sector development agents. Substantial borrowing by the government to finance its budget deficits has increased interest rates, thus discouraging bank investment in relatively risky long-term business ventures.

POLICY AND STRATEGY IMPLICATIONS

The previous conclusions carry implications for export sector policy and strategy formulations. At the macropolicy level, it is evident that developing countries require the formulation and committed implementation of coherent national export policies. Policymakers therefore require better insight into the perceived constraints of their exporter and nonexporter firms and the prevailing systems of operation that influence their behaviors. Areas requiring immediate attention include the following:

1. The existing network processes and the roles that they play in market information acquisition and dissemination, as well as the creation of joint resources for reducing marketing costs. A better understanding of the system will provide ideas for policy interventions aimed at strengthening the networks.
2. The manpower capacity of the exporting firms and their manpower requirements. As indicated earlier, cross-border trade may be seriously constrained by exporters' inadequate knowledge of business practices in the neighboring countries as well as inadequate language skills (cf Dichtl, Koglmayr, and Mueller, 1990). Policy interventions that provide export business trainees with requisite language skills and business knowledge must be considered. It is also worth considering the establish-

ment of export promotion offices in neighboring countries to help neophyte exporters make contacts with key business networks in the countries.

3. The financial constraint. Government policies of mopping up scanty local savings through the issuing of treasury bonds must be reviewed. The establishment of special financial institutions (such as the Export Finance Company in Ghana) to provide medium- and long-term investment funds to producer-exporters must be considered in other countries. Such financial institutions may also contribute to proper export risk management of the exporters through the creation of export guarantee schemes.

4. Contract enforcement mechanisms. As the Ghanaian evidence showed, weak domestic supply may produce a business culture characterized by contract flexibility, i.e., high tolerance of poor contractual performance. Local suppliers may use the low level of economic development and infrastructural shortcomings as excuses for delays in delivery and payment. To reduce the "spillover" effect of such negative practices on relationships between exporters and foreign buyers, policy interventions may be needed to instill higher levels of contractual discipline in local business practices. Furthermore, following Fafchamps (1996), it is purposeful for governments to design systems in which third-party inspection of export products takes place prior to their shipment. This will discourage overseas buyers from disputing shipments on arrival, thereby delaying payment or forcing developing country exporters into granting discounts.

It is important, however, for policymakers to bear in mind that export assistance must complement rather than replace strategies pursued by firms collectively at the industry level or individually at the firm level. At the industry level, firms can engage in joint resource creation and sharing through collaborations within their industry networks. Although the Ghanaian study did not produce evidence of industrial district formation, the formation of product associations provides a framework for joint resource creation by firms facing similar constraints to export performance. Elsewhere in Africa (for example, the horticultural subsector in the East African countries of Kenya and Uganda), there is some evidence of incipient industrial districts. As Harris-Pascal, Humphrey, and Dolan (1998) found in their study of the buyer-driven commodity chain within the horticultural sector, supermarkets would like producer-exporters of fresh fruits and vegetables to invest in facilities such as greenhouses, cooling and cold-storage transport, as well as on-site packaging equipment in order to deliver the quality of products demanded by European consumers. Since such investments are outside the means of a single small producer-exporter, the market is likely to be dominated by large-scale producer-exporters. Joint investments and other intraindustry collaborative arrangements are required to offset trends of concentration within the sector. Similar arguments can be made for other export sectors dominated by small-scale producer-exporters.

On the strength of these discussions, we argued in favor of the development of a new conceptual framework for studying the internationalization processes of companies located in developing countries. We proposed that an internationalization process should be seen from both upstream and downstream perspectives. The argument here is that most neophyte exporters from developing countries require "parenting" links with suppliers and distributors in the developed countries through which their managerial and technical capacities can be upgraded. These links will also help reduce risks and anxieties that the new entrepreneurs might experience in connection with their initial export efforts.

Contrary to previous perspectives on internationalization, we argued that upstream internationalization, for example, through supplier arrangements and strategic alliances, must be highly encouraged in these countries. Government institutions must also be encouraged to develop an enabling environment for such alliances. Upstream internationalization, however, is not without problems. Developed country companies that enter into long-term relations with developing country companies are likely to demand control over aspects of the management decisions and operations of the developing country companies. This is to protect them from unpleasant surprises involving changes in production methods and management practices that may contribute to reducing the value of their investment. In the absence of such controls, the collaborating companies may be compelled to engage in continuous haggling and negotiations that will weaken the mutual trust and benefits that may arise from such collaborations.

DIRECTIONS FOR FURTHER STUDIES

The discussions in this study highlighted the paucity of research into the internationalization processes of developing country firms. Doubtlessly, substantial research is required, not only in Ghana, but also in other developing economies, for us to begin to gain an informed understanding of the opportunities and challenges that these firms face in the next century. To conclude this chapter, we consider it purposeful to emphasize some of the research issues that require attention.

Integration of Theory and Context

The contextual embeddedness of entrepreneurial activities needs to be recognized in international business theory formulation. The limited applicability of existing theories to developing country situations derives partly from this omission. The issue of contextuality is further complicated by the fact that internationalization entails interfirm relations across frequently disparate contexts. Such interactions inspire changes in the various national contexts, thereby producing a dynamic process. Firms in technology- and knowledge-dependent situations (as most developing country-based firms are) will experience tremendous demands for change in their business behavior from firms abroad. The impact of this diversity of stimuli and specific behavioral adaptation requirements should be a subject of vigorous research in the future. Such studies should be guided by the awareness that context is neither a static nor an objective concept; it is constantly changing through actions, reactions, and interpretations of the actors (firms, organizations, and institutions) in their daily encounters. In this regard, each firm may define the context differently due to the perception and action possibilities of their managers and workers and the issues with which they are confronted. Extant theories of internationalization are presented, however, either as context free (i.e., they assume that the theory is relevant in all types of contexts), or the context is not specified, but appears as a general environment including economic, social, and cultural forces.

Future research needs to integrate context into the theories of internationalization by identifying the contextual actors and institutions. For example, export promotion agencies regulate, facilitate, and conduct activities on behalf of companies. They must therefore not be conceived as factors outside the company; they are partners and must be part and parcel of a theory. In a similar way, other contextual institutions must be made visible and, as actors, integrated into theories of internationalization. Inspirations to this line of study can be found in theories of the network approach and government-business relations as well as studies of industrial districts and recent works on business systems (Whitley, 1994).

Country-Specific Systems of Government-Business Partnership

The debate on the creation of an enabling environment for export sector development tends to assume the existence of a set of universal attributes that, if available, will serve as catalysts for the internationalization of firms. Building on the view that a variety of successful national recipes exist for business development, it can be argued that each country must devise the set of support mechanisms that can effectively promote the internationalization of its businesses. These country-specific support schemes must be based on the historical evolution of businesses in each country and on the relationships between entrepreneurs and public institutions. We have already stressed the need for dialogue and partnership mechanisms that can coordinate efforts made by businesses and government institutions.

Existing theories, however, tend to either omit the government and its institutions or to regard them as a power over and above business—a power that stipulates the free space for business actions. Future research needs to explicitly include government-business relations in the theories of how companies internationalize. However, as government is part of the context of the business community, there is no universal model for government-business relations. These relations emerge over time, shaped by the practices and experiences of both business and government. Only by confronting empirical findings in specific countries with theoretical modeling can the relationship between government and business be understood. In Ghana, we found that the present perspective of government supremacy is being replaced gradually by a Partnership Model based on open dialogue between loosely coordinated public institutions and the companies and their associations.

Business Repositioning and Strategic Focus in Upstream Internationalization

The short history of the business systems in most developing countries and the already global economy into which the companies are to be integrated need to be recognized in the formulation of theories of internationalization.

As previously argued, existing theories of internationalization focus on the downstream, i.e., the export route, to becoming international. This route may be feasible for companies from developing countries when entering neighboring countries, i.e., those with a similar context and background as the country in question, provided that the institutional arrangement and the infrastructure are conducive to cross-border transactions. However, the available theories do not provide much insight and guidance for companies aiming at entering or penetrating already global industries in mature market economies. Future research must study internationalization within a broader conceptual framework. We proposed that the internationalization processes of companies from developing countries be seen from both upstream and downstream perspectives. By focusing on the upstream route, companies will be able to upgrade their technology and management style and thus create a platform for a potential downstream internationalization, while consolidating their business in the domestic market.

Obviously, an upstream route to integration into the global economy may require management to refocus. One of the observations made about Ghanaian export businesses is that the owners have different business interests. Many of them run two or three businesses concurrently, despite the limited financial and managerial resources at their disposal. It can be imagined that upstream business relations, especially with technology suppliers in the industrialized countries, will compel some of the entrepreneurs to change and concentrate their resources on the "core" product they are to develop in collaboration with their foreign partners. With a clarity of strategic intent, it may be easier to identify core competencies that should form the focus of their collaboration.

Our present knowledge about how these relationships emerge, their contents, and the strategic consequences is very rudimentary and fragmentary. We are currently engaged in a longitudinal study of such relationships between ten selected Ghanaian and Danish firms. Several similar studies are required in the future in both Ghana and other African countries for us to improve our insight into core competence transfers between developed and developing country firms.

CONCLUSIONS

The discussions in this book have shown that the extant literature on the internationalization process of companies has focused attention on downstream routes of internationalization, addressing issues such as motives for exporting, stages in the export market expansion process, profiles of firms associated with specific export stages, and factors determining the progression from one stage to another (Leonidou and Katsikeas, 1996). These issues have been discussed in the Stages Models, Contingency Models, and (Inter)-Action Models presented in Chapter 1. The main objective of this book is to explore the relevance of these theories and models to the study of the internationalization process of developing country-based companies. As shown in Chapter 6, developing country companies are not likely to preface their internationalization process with domestic market involvement, as suggested in the Stages Models. The models' assumption of gradual experiential learning about overseas markets is, however, relevant to an understanding of the internationalization process of such companies. The empirical evidence from Ghana corroborates this viewpoint. Chapter 9 showed that Ghanaian exporting firms tend to have little or no domestic market experience prior to their decisions to engage in exporting. But as explained in the Transaction Costs Theory, the limited experience of these companies aggravates their sense of uncertainty about their international business activities. They seek to reduce these uncertainties through collaborative arrangements with overseas customers, as suggested by the (Inter)Action Models. Developed country importers, on the other hand, are likely to exhibit opportunistic behaviors by capitalizing on their market knowledge advantages and the inability of their developing country suppliers to monitor the transactions closely. Exporting is therefore a highly risky business undertaking for companies from developing countries. As a result, they depend on government support to establish solid foundations for their growth.

With regard to motives underlying companies' decisions to embark on exports, the empirical results show that Ghanaian companies are motivated primarily by opportunities to earn foreign currency. Through a government-initiated foreign currency retention scheme, the exporting companies enjoy some degree of flexibility and control over the importation of their inputs and equipment. Some Ghanaian importers have diversified into export trading to finance their import business. Foreign exchange acquisition may therefore remain an important motive for developing country companies due to the perennial shortage of hard currency in these countries. The study, therefore, provides an empirical endorsement of foreign currency retention schemes during the initial stages of export sector development in developing countries.

The general understanding that companies are basically reactive during the early stages of their export development process has not been supported in this study. The commitment of the governments in developing countries to export sector development and the establishment of a wide range of promotional institutions and incentive packages to encourage export are definitely important motivators. It is wrong, however, to assume that developing country companies are passive recipients of subsidies and assistance. The Ghanaian evidence shows that even small companies tend to take initiatives in locating distributors abroad, either through business visits as follow-ups on information from friends or through participation in trade fairs and exhibitions to present their products to potential buyers. Granting their resource capacity limitations, these efforts must be seen as a reflection of a strong managerial urge to success in their business endeavors. The preparedness of the firms to venture abroad and their choice of market, however, depend on the degree of added value of the export products. Whereas manufacturing and processing companies tend to target the domestic market during the initial stages of their operations, exporters of fresh food items and nonprocessed products normally start exporting in the first year of their establishment.

The evidence also shows that undercapitalization is a major constraint for the exporting companies, a natural consequence of their small sizes and family ownership. The harsh credit conditions and the risk-averse attitudes of the local banks tend to contribute negatively to the problem. Exporters in many other developing countries are likely to experience similar problems. The results in this study therefore provide additional confirmation for the view that financial support is crucial to firms in the early stages of their export process. Policy instruments aimed at creating venture capitals (from both internal and external sources) to support committed and deserving exporters are therefore worth serious attention.

We have also argued that a downstream route of internationalization presents only a partial framework for understanding the process by which developing country firms are integrated into the world economy. Upstream internationalization has been suggested as a supplement to the mainstream perspective. By studying both upstream and downstream internationalization processes of Ghanaian firms, the present study makes two important contributions to our knowledge about internationalization of firms. First, it shows that firms strengthen their competitive positions in the global market, not only by improving their marketing activities and relationships with their foreign customers, but also through links with their foreign suppliers (i.e., the procurement side of internationalization). Thus, upstream and downstream internationalization are of equal importance in the integration of national economies into the global economy. Second, manufacturing companies in countries such as Ghana seek opportunities to enter into strategic alliances with suppliers of technology and inputs abroad. These upstream arrangements strengthen their technological and organizational capabilities and enable them to raise their product and marketing efforts to international standards. Thus, upstream internationalization prepares these firms for downstream internationalization.

Keeping in mind the general limitations of results from a single country study and a small sample, we believe the results of this study offer interesting implications for international business management as well as for national economic policies for developing countries. Companies engaged in downstream internationalization may do well to supplement their efforts with the management of their upstream value chain through links with foreign firms. Furthermore, national export promotion policies must be replaced by international business promotion policies embracing both upstream and downstream aspects of internationalization. Upstream-internationalizing companies produce technological and managerial knowledge and thereby improve the quality of their products. These products may become inputs to downstream-internationalizing companies and help raise the added value of the export products. In addition to this, one can expect interfirm spillover of knowledge and skills where upstream-internationalizing companies collaborate with other companies in industrial clusters. This will then create a seedbed for the emergence of exporting companies with higher competitive advantages.

Appendix A

Dominant Contingency Models of Internationalization

THE TRANSACTION COSTS THEORY

The Transaction Costs Theory stipulates the conditions under which a company will, or should, choose to use the market, e.g., an agent or importer, or when it will, or should, internalize the activities of the company by, for example, establishing a production subsidiary abroad.

The theory stipulates that if

1. uncertainty about outcomes prevails,
2. transactions recur frequently, and
3. transactions require substantial transaction-specific investments,

then

> the economic activity will be internalized, i.e., carried out by the company itself rather than transacted using the markets.

This behavior occurs because companies and their managers are characterized by bounded rationality and have opportunistic inclinations. For these reasons, companies decide to "produce the products themselves" rather than buy them from the market (Williamson, 1979, 1981; Douma and Schreuder, 1991).

The three conditions are often met in export business operations. First, the outcomes of export businesses are uncertain. Second, export transactions are, in most cases, repetitive. Third, exporters very often adapt to specific market conditions and thus make market- or transaction-specific investments. Due to high marketing costs, however, exporters may resort to the use of channel members rather than undertaking all their marketing activities by themselves.

The Eclectic Paradigm of FDIs

Another Contingency Model is the Eclectic Paradigm for foreign direct investments (FDIs), developed by Dunning (1993a, 1995). The paradigm explains the conditions under which a company internationalizes through FDIs rather than by exporting. Thus, it shares the same basic idea with the Transaction Costs Theory and also explains the growth and development of multinational companies. In the Eclectic Paradigm, three conditions are required for an FDI to take place—the so-called OLI formula. For an FDI to occur, a company must enjoy the following:

- *Ownership advantages,* i.e., proprietary rights, e.g., a patent that provides the firm with a competitive advantage. An ownership advantage is necessary to overcome the basic advantages a naturalized company has in its home market. Thus, an ownership advantage is a precondition for going international.
- *Location-specific advantages,* i.e., advantages derived from superior factor or demand endowments in the foreign country. The location-specific advantage is a precondition for establishing production abroad, whether by way of license or investment in a production subsidiary.
- *Internalization advantages,* i.e., advantages derived from doing it yourself instead of relying on the market system. In case a market does not exist for a particular product, or the price offered is too low compared to the company's own estimates of its potential, or, as in case of a license, the company cannot control its use, then the company may decide to establish its own production or sales subsidiary abroad. Thus, an internalization advantage is the precondition for investing abroad.

The three preconditions can be arranged in the form of a table of conditions under which various market entry modes will prevail.

This scheme is presented in Table A. The Eclectic Paradigm thus outlines the contingencies that influence an international firm's choice of foreign market entry strategy. If a foreign country possesses advantageous factor endowments and local firms exist to exploit them, the international firm may explore opportunities for using licensing as an entry strategy. However, if local firms are incapable of using the international firm's know-how, the latter may establish production facilities to take advantage of the local factor endowments.

TABLE A. The Eclectic Paradigm: Conditions for an FDI

	Exports	**License**	**Foreign Direct Investment**
Ownership Advantages	+	+	+
Location-Specific Advantages	–	+	+
Internalization Advantages	–	–	+

Appendix B

Firms That Participated in the Study

Name of Firm	Year of Estab- lishment	Products
1. Accra Brewery Ltd.	1931	Beer
2. Adicopa Farms	1987	Fresh pineapples
3. Alfus (Gh.) Ltd.	1987	Fresh yams
4. Aluworks	1985	Aluminium plates
5. Astek Fruit Processing Ltd.	1983	Fruit juice drink
6. Baffour Sencherey Ltd.	1970	Fresh yams
7. Cashew & Spices Products Ltd.	1990	Cashew nuts
8. Combined Farmers Ltd.	1977	Fresh pineapples
9. Getrade (Gh.) Ltd.	1987	Handicrafts
10. Kassardjian (Gh.) Ltd.	1958	Shea nuts
11. Kiku Company Ltd.	1983	Fresh shrimp
12. Modern Optical Works	1970	Cattle horns
13. Nulux Plantations Ltd.	1986	Cottonseed
14. Packrite Industries	1987	Paper cartons and packaging
15. Poly Products (Gh.) Ltd.	1977	Polythene bags
16. Scanstyle Ltd.	1978	Textiles
17. Spintex Ltd.	1971	Kila nuts
18. Sulleyman Company Ltd.	1968	Common salt
19. Wadeye Company Ltd.	1988	Furniture parts
20. Woody Ltd.	1977	Panel doors

Appendix C

Product Associations in Operation As of December 1995

1. Coffee and Shea Nuts Exporters Association

2. Federation of Ghanaian Jewelers

3. Game and Wildlife Exporters Association

4. Ghana Assorted Foodstuffs Exporters Association

5. Ghana Furniture Producers Association

6. Ghana Palm Oil, Palm Kernel Oil, and Coconut Oil Exporters Association

7. Ghana Yam Exporters Association

8. Handicraft Exporters Association

9. Horticulturists Association of Ghana

10. National Association of Kola Nut Dealers

11. Organization for Export Development of Seafood

12. Salt Exporters Association

13. Non-Ferrous Scrap Metal Exporters Association

14. Vegetable Exporters Association

Appendix D

Survey Questionnaire

COMPANY BACKGROUND

(Respondent: The founder of the business)

1. When did you conceive the idea of starting the company?

2. Why did you want to enter this kind of business?

3. Did you have any previous business experience when starting this company?

COMPANY PROFILE

1. Year of commencement

2. Legal status/ownership form

   ❑ Limited-liability company

   ❑ Partnership

   ❑ Other (specify)

3. Links with other companies

   ❑ A subsidiary of another Ghanaian company (specify)

   ❑ A subsidiary of a foreign company (specify)

4. Current product portfolio

Products	% of total sales	Export's share of total sales
1._____	_____	_____
2._____	_____	_____
3._____	_____	_____

5. Have there been new additions and/or eliminations in the product portfolio during the last three years?

❑ No

❑ Yes

If yes, what are the new additions?

6. Give reasons for this change.

7. (a) What proportion of your total sales goes to final consumers?

(b) What proportion goes to institutions, businesses, and other organizations?

(c) Has there been any change in these proportions during the last three years?

❑   No

❑   Yes

If yes, explain how and why.

8. In rough estimates, what were your total sales during the following years:

1991:

1992:

1993:

9. Number of employees:

	1991	Present
Senior/top management		
Men	_____	_____
Women	_____	_____
Middle-level management		
Men	_____	_____
Women	_____	_____
Junior management		
Men	_____	_____
Women	_____	_____
Other administrative staff		
Men	_____	_____
Women	_____	_____
Workers		
Men	_____	_____
Women	_____	_____

TECHNOLOGY AND CAPACITY UTILIZATION

1. Did you purchase all brand-new production equipment when you started?

2. Have you changed any major production equipment during the last three years?

3. What are the reasons for the new investments?

4. How did you finance the new equipment?

5. How do you assess the capacity utilization of your production equipment today?

   ❑ Full-capacity utilization

   ❑ 75-100% utilization

   ❑ 50-75% utilization

   ❑ Less than 50% utilization

6. Have you undertaken any other major investments during the last three years?

   ❑ No

   ❑ Yes

7. Have you increased or decreased the number of employees in your company during the last 3 years?

   ❑ No

   ❑ Yes

   If yes, by how many?

ORGANIZATION
AND HUMAN RESOURCE DEVELOPMENT

To the interviewer:

- Ask for a copy of the company's organizational chart and discuss the structure with the respondent.
- Find out if there is a marketing department on the chart. If there is, discuss the tasks of this department.
- Discuss how the company organizes its export operations.

Questions:

1. Do you have a specific training program for your managerial staff?

2. Do workers have a specific training program?

3. How do you make sure you have the most qualified staff working for you?

4. How do you motivate both managers and workers?

INTERNATIONALIZATION PROCESS

1. How did you get your first export order?

2. When was this?

3. Which products did you export on the first occasion?

4. Which country did you export to?

5. What was your primary motivation to start the export business?

6. How much of your total annual exports still goes to this country?

7. Describe the growth of your exports over the years.

   (a) Did the number of countries you sold to increase rapidly or gradually?

   (b) Which countries do you sell to currently?

   (c) When did you start exporting to each of these countries?

   (d) Which of your products do you export to each country?

   (e) How much (in cedis) do you export to each of these countries?

8. Do you sell to importers in any of the countries, or do you sell through agents?

9. Do you sell to more than one importer/distributor in any of these countries?

10. Do you have a sales office in any of these countries?

    (a) If yes, what are the major functions of the sales office?

    (b) How many people do you employ in sales offices abroad?

11. Can you tell me the reasons underlying your choice of distribution (sales) method in each of the countries?

12. How do you obtain customers in new countries?

13. Why do you use this approach to find new customers in new countries?

14. What proportion (%) of your total sales comes from exports?

15. Has the proportion been higher than this in any of the previous years?

    (a) If yes, what was the highest proportion (%)?

    (b) What are the reasons for the decline?

EXPORT ORGANIZATION AND STRATEGIES

1. Do you have a sales or marketing department?

2. (a) Do you have an export department as well?

   (b) If no, who is in charge of your export transactions?

3. What are the major duties of those in charge of the export?

4. What are the qualifications of these people?

5. How long have they been with the company?

6. Did any of them have export experience before joining the company?

7. How do you decide on the price (free on board [FOB]) of your products?

8. Are the prices the same in each country?

EXPORT INFORMATION AND EXPORT ASSISTANCE

1. What kind of information do you use in your export decisions?

2. Where do you get the information?

3. Do you get all the information you need?

4. How do you assess Ghanaian government institutions (e.g., the Ghana Export Promotion Council) as a source of information?

5. Have you ever approached foreign embassies in Ghana for information?

(a) If yes, what kind of information did you ask for?

(b) Which embassies have you approached?

(c) What were their reactions to your request?

6. What other kinds of assistance do you get from the following:

(a) Ghanaian government organizations

(b) Foreign embassies and organizations

EXPORT PROBLEMS AND PLANS

1. What have been the major problems you have faced in your export business?

2. How have you solved them?

3. Which problems do you face now?

4. What difficulties do Ghanaian exporters of your type of products face?

5. What, in your opinion, should be done to minimize these difficulties?

6. Do exporters in your line of business have any associations?

(a) What are the functions of these associations?

(b) Are you a member of these associations?

Notes

Introduction

1. Eriksson, Johanson, Majkgård, and Sharma (1997) distinguish between two kinds of overseas market knowledge: (1) foreign business knowledge (i.e., knowledge about clients, markets, and competition) and (2) foreign institutional knowledge (i.e., knowledge of governments, institutional framework, rules, and culture).

Chapter 1

1. This model is usually referred to in international business literature as the "Stages Model." The change in terminology here is to emphasize the learning dimension of the model.

2. For details, see Appendix A: Dominant Contingency Models of Internationalization.

Chapter 3

1. There are plans to extend the private-sector program to other assistance recipient countries in the future.

Chapter 4

1. Promotion activities and the determination of prices have caught much less theoretical and practical attention. In practice, promotion is often considered in conjunction with entry mode decisions and operations, especially when personal selling is the primary promotion tool. Pricing, although crucial to the success of international undertakings, is often made by simply using the cost-plus pricing (markup pricing) formula.

Chapter 5

1. Some researchers see the network as the dominant governance structure of the future. Michalet (1991) thus talks of "the contractual economy," and Dunning

(1995) introduces the concept of "alliance capitalism" in place of "hierarchical capitalism."

2. We prefer to use the term "theory of relationship" rather than "theory of proximity," as the development of communication technology is eroding the need for physical proximity of firms and institutions.

Chapter 7

1. A three-year rolling public investment program was introduced in 1986 for the purpose of streamlining government expenditures.

2. The main nontraditional products exported in 1997 included fresh fruits and vegetables (e.g., pineapples, avocados, bananas, kola nuts, and cashew nuts), furniture and other wood products, fish and fish products, aluminium products, and cocoa butter.

3. A modification in the classification of products has increased the share of nontraditional exports since 1995. Using the old classification, exports in 1997 would amount to barely 10.5 percent of the total value of exports.

4. In 1998, the downward trend was reversed, with growth recorded at 5.3 percent (Government of Ghana, 1999).

5. Government figures put industry growth rates at 4.1 percent in 1995, 4.8 percent in 1996, and 6.4 percent in 1997 (Government of Ghana, 1999).

Chapter 9

1. *Kente* is a traditional Ghanaian fabric (usually handwoven) in bright colors. It has become fairly popular among some African-American communities in the United States as a symbol of African roots and identity.

Chapter 12

1. The viability of this approach to exporting depends, however, on the opportunities available for ethnic business establishment in the major export markets of countries belonging to the Organization for Economic Cooperation and Development (OECD).

Bibliography

Albaum, G., Strandskov, J., Duerr, E., and Dowd, L. (1994). *International Marketing and Export Management* (Addison-Wesley Publishing Company, Wokingham, England).

Anderson, E. and Gatignon, H. (1986). "Modes of Foreign Entry: A Transaction Cost Analysis and Propositions," *Journal of International Business Studies,* Vol. 17, No. 4, pp. 1-26.

Asenso-Okyere, W.K. and Yahaya, K. (1993). "International Trade and Payments," in Nyanteng, V.K. (Ed.), *Policies and Options for Ghanaian Economic Development* (The Institute of Statistical, Social and Economic Research, Legon, Ghana), pp. 46-67.

Baah-Nuakoh, A., Jebuni, C.D., Oduro, A.D., and Asante, Y. (1996). *Exporting Manufactures from Ghana: Is Adjustment Enough?* (Overseas Development Institute and University of Ghana, London).

Berent, P.H. (1976). "International Research Is Different: The Case for Centralised Control," *Proceedings from Seminar on International Marketing Research—Does It Provide What the User Needs?* (ESOMAR, Amsterdam), pp. 110-121.

Berger, P.L. and Luckman, T. (1966). *The Social Construction of Reality* (Pengiun, London).

Bilkey, W.J. (1978). "An Attempted Integration of the Literature on the Export Behaviour of Firms," *Journal of International Business Studies,* Vol. 9, No. 1, pp. 33-46.

Bilkey, W.J. and Tesar, G. (1977). "The Export Behavior of Smaller-Sized Wisconsin Manufacturing Firms," *Journal of International Business Studies,* Vol. 8, No. 2, pp. 93-98.

Bohn, K., Carlsen, J., Fast, M., and Sørensen, O.J. (1989). *Virksomhedens Internationalisering-En Undersøgelse af 20 Virksomheder i Hadsund Kommune* (Internationale Studier, Aalborg Universitetscenter, Aalborg, Denmark).

Bonaccorsi, A. (1992). "On the Relationship Between Firm Size and Export Intensity," *Journal of International Business,* Vol. 23, No. 4, pp. 605-635.

Borys, B. and Jemison, B.D. (1989). "Hybrid Arrangements As Strategic Alliances: Theoretical Issues in Organizational Combinations," *Academy of Management Journal,* Vol. 114, No. 2, pp. 234-249.

Buckley, J.P. (1988). "The Limits of Explanation: Testing the Internationalization Theory of the Multinational Enterprise," *Journal of International Business Studies,* Vol. 19, No. 2, pp. 181-193.

Buckley, J.P. (1990). "Problems and Development in the Core Theory of International Business," *Journal of International Business Studies,* Vol. 21, No. 4, pp. 657-666.

Burt, R.S. (1992). "The Social Structure of Competition," in Nohria, N. and Eccles, R.G. (Eds.), *Networks and Organizations* (Harvard Business School Press, Boston), pp. 57-91.

Calof, J. (1993). "The Mode Choice and Change Decision Process and Its Impact on International Performance," *International Business Review,* Vol. 2, No. 1, pp. 97-119.

Cavusgil, S.T. (1980). "On the Internationalization Process of Firms," *European Research*, Vol. 8, No. 4, pp. 273-281.

Cavusgil, S.T. (1982). "Some Observations on the Relevance of Critical Variables for Internationalization Stages," in Czinkota, M.R. and Tesar, G. (Eds.), *Export Management: An International Context* (Praeger, New York), pp. 276-285.

Cavusgil, S.T. (1984a). "Differences Among Exporting Firms Based on Degree of Internationalization," *Journal of Business Research*, Vol. 12, No. 3, pp. 195-208.

Cavusgil, S.T. (1984b). "International Marketing Research: Insights into Company Practices," *Research in Marketing*, Vol. 7, No. 2, pp. 261-288.

Cavusgil, S.T., Bilkey, W.J., and Tesar, G. (1979). "A Note on the Export Behavior of Firms: Exporter Profiles," *Journal of International Business Studies,* Vol. 10, No. 2, pp. 91-97.

Cavusgil, S.T. and Naor, J. (1987). "Firm and Management Characteristics As Discriminators of Export Marketing Activity," *Journal of Business Research,* Vol. 15, No. 3, pp. 221-235.

Cavusgil, S.T. and Nevin, J.R. (1981). "Internal Determinants of Export Marketing Behavior: An Empirical Investigation," *Journal of Marketing Research*, Vol. 28, No. 1, pp. 114-119.

Chao, P. (1993). "Partitioning Country-of-Origin Effects: Consumer Evaluation of Hybrid Products," *Journal of International Business Studies*, Vol. 24, No. 2, pp. 291-306.

Christensen, P.R. and Overgaard, B.B. (1990). "Export Expansion and Change in the Acquiring of Information in SMEs." A paper delivered at the sixteenth European International Business Association (EIBA) annual conference, Madrid.

Coase, R.H. (1937). "The Nature of the Firm," *Economica,* Vol. 4, pp. 386-405; reprinted in Stigler, G.J. and Boulding, K.S. (Eds.) (1952), *Readings in Price Theory* (Irwin, Homewood, Illinois), pp. 331-351.

Cohen, M.D. and Sproull, L.S. (Eds.). (1996). *Organizational Learning* (Sage, London).

Cooper, R.G. and Kleinschmidt, E.J. (1985). "The Impact of Export Strategy on Export Sales Performance," *Journal of International Business Studies,* Vol. 16, No. 1, pp. 37-55.

Cundiff, W.E. and Hilger, M.T. (1988). *Marketing in the International Environment,* Second Edition (Prentice-Hall International, Inc., Englewood Cliffs, New Jersey).

Czinkota, M.R. and Ricks, D.A. (1983). "The Use of a Multi-Measurement Approach in the Determination of Company Export Priorities," *Journal of the Academy of Marketing Sciences,* Vol. 11, No. 3, pp. 283-291.

Czinkota, M.R. and Ricks, D.A. (1994). "Export Assistance: Are We Supporting the Best Programs?" In Czinkota, Michael R. and Ronkainen, I.A. (Eds.), *International Marketing Strategy: Environmental Assessment and Entry Strategies* (The Dryden Press, Florida), pp. 63-72.

Czinkota, M.R. and Ronkainen, I.A. (1990). *International Marketing,* Second Edition (The Dryden Press, Chicago).

Danish International Development Assistance (DANIDA) (1995). *Capital Fund for SMEs in Ghana* (Aalborg University, Aalborg, Denmark).

Das, M. (1994). "Successful and Unsuccessful Exporters from Developing Countries: Some Preliminary Findings," *European Journal of Marketing,* Vol. 29, No. 12, pp. 19-33.

Deshpande, R. and Zaltman, G. (1982). "Factors Affecting the Use of Market Research Information: A Path Analysis," *Journal of Marketing Research,* Vol. 19, No. 1, pp. 14-31.

Diamantopoulos, A., Schlegelmilch, B.B., and Allpress, C. (1990). "Export Marketing Research in Practice: A Comparison of Users and Non-Users," *Journal of Marketing Management,* Vol. 6, No. 3, pp. 257-273.

Diamantopoulos, A., Schlegelmilch, B.B., and Kathy, K.Y.T. (1993). "Understanding the Role of Export Marketing Assistance: Empirical Evidence and Research Needs," *European Journal of Marketing,* Vol. 27, No. 4, pp. 5-18.

Dichtl, E., Koglmayr, H.-G., and Mueller, S. (1990). "International Orientation As a Pre-Condition for Export Success," *Journal of International Business Studies,* Vol. 21, No. 1, pp. 23-40.

Douglas, S.P. and Craig, C.S. (1983). *International Marketing Research* (Prentice-Hall International Inc., Englewood Cliffs, New Jersey).

Douma, S. and Schreuder, H. (1991). *Economic Approaches to Organizations* (Prentice-Hall, London), pp. 124-150.

Doz, Y. (1991). "Partnership in Europe: The Soft Restructuring Option?" in Mattsson, I.G. and Stymne, B. (Eds.), *Corporate and Industry Strategies for Europe* (Elsevier Science Publishers B.V., Amsterdam, The Netherlands), pp. 303-326.

Drucker, P.F. (1958). "Marketing and Economic Development," *Journal of Marketing,* Vol. 23, No. 3, pp. 252-259.

Dunning, J.H. (1988). *Explaining International Production* (Unwin Hyman, London).

Dunning, J.H. (1989). "The Study of International Business: A Plea for a More Interdisciplinary Approach," *Journal of International Business Studies,* Vol. 20, No. 3, pp. 411-436.

Dunning, J.H. (1993a). *The Globalization of Business* (Routledge, London).

Dunning, J.H. (1993b). *Multinational Enterprises and the Global Economy* (Addison-Wesley Publishing Company, Wokingham, England).

Dunning, J.H. (1995). "Reappraising the Eclectic Paradigm in the Age of Alliance Capitalism," *Journal of International Business,* Vol. 26, No. 3, pp. 461-491.

Economic Intelligence Unit (EIU) (1991). *Ghana: Country Profile (1989-1990)* (EIU, London).

Ellis, J. and Williams, D. (1995). *International Business Strategy* (Pitman Publishing, London).

Eriksson, K., Johanson, J., Majkgård, A., and Sharma, D.D. (1997). "Experiential Knowledge and Cost in the Internationalization Process," *Journal of International Business Studies*, Vol. 28, No. 2, pp. 337-360.

Fafchamps, M. (1996). "The Enforcement of Commercial Contracts in Ghana" *World Development*, Vol. 24, No. 3, pp. 427-448.

Fahey, L. and King, W.R. (1977). "Environmental Scanning for Corporate Planning," *Business Horizons*, pp. 61-71.

Faulkner, D. (1995). *International Strategic Alliances: Co-operating to Compete* (McGraw-Hill, London).

Feldman, M.S. and March, J.G. (1981). "Information in Organizations As Signal and Symbol," *Administrative Science Quarterly*, Vol. 26, No. 2, pp. 171-186.

Ferguson, P.R. and Ferguson, G.J. (1994). *Industrial Economies* (Macmillan, London).

Fiol, C.M. and Huff, A.S. (1992). "Maps for Managers: Where Are We? Where Do We Go from Here?" *Journal of Management Studies*, Vol. 29, No. 3, pp. 267-285.

Ford, D. (1997). *Understanding Business Markets* (Dryden, London).

Forsgren, M., Holm, U., and Johanson J. (1992). "Internationalization of the Second Degree: The Emergence of European-Based Centres in Swedish Firms," in Young, S. and Hamill, J. (Eds.), *Europe and the Multinationals* (Edward Elgar, Aldershot, England), pp. 235-253.

Ghana Export Promotion Council (1995). *Export Performance—Non-Traditional Products* (GEPC, Accra, Ghana).

Goodwin, J.B. (1993). "The Current Account Deficit," *The Journal of Management Studies*, Vol. 9, No. 1, pp. 54-64.

Government of Ghana (1999). *Budget Statement and Economic Policy of the Government of Ghana for the 1999 Financial Year* (Assembly Press, Accra, Ghana), pp. 1-79.

Granovetter, M. and Swedberg, R. (Eds.). (1992). *The Sociology of Economic Life* (Westview Press, Boulder, Colorado).

Green, R.H. (1987). *Ghana: Stabilization and Adjustment Programmes and Policies* (World Institute for Development Economics Research, Helsinki, Finland).

Green, R.T. and White, P.D. (1976). "Methodological Considerations in Cross-National Consumer Research," *Journal of International Business Studies*, Vol. 7, No. 1, pp. 81-87.

Gundlach, G.T., Achrol R., and Mentzer, J.T. (1995). "The Structure of Commitment in Exchange," *Journal of Marketing*, Vol. 59, No. 1, pp. 78-92.

Håkansson, H. and Johanson, J. (1993). "The Network As a Governance Structure: Interfirm Cooperation Beyond Markets and Hierarchies," in Grabher, G. (Ed.), *The Embedded Firm* (Routledge, London), pp. 35-51.

Hamilton, G. and Biggart, N.W. (1988). "Markets, Culture and Authority: A Comparative Analysis of Management and Organization in the Far East," *American Journal of Sociology*, Vol. 94, Supplement, pp. 552-594.

Harris-Pascal, C., Humphrey, J., and Dolan, C. (1998). "Value Chains and Upgrading the Impact of U.K. Retailers on the Fresh Fruit and Vegetable Industry in Africa." Paper presented at workshop on businesses in development at Copenhagen, October 1-2.

Hedberg, B. (1981). "How Organizations Learn and Unlearn," in Nyström, P.C. and Starbuck, W.J. (Eds.), *Handbook of Organizational Design,* Volume 1 (Oxford University Press, New York), pp. 3-27.

Holbert, N. (1974). "How Managers See Marketing Research," *Journal of Advertising Research,* Vol. 14, No. 6, pp. 41-46.

Hollensen, S. (1998). *Global Marketing: A Market-Responsive Approach* (Prentice-Hall, London).

Huq, M.M. (1989). *The Economy of Ghana: The First 25 Years Since Independence* (Macmillan Press, London).

Hutchful, E. (1994). *Structural Adjustment in Ghana: An Evaluation* (Department of African Studies, Wayne State University, Detroit, Michigan).

Institute of Statistical, Social, and Economic Research (ISSER) (1996). *The State of the Ghanaian Economy in 1995* (University of Ghana, Legon).

Institute of Statistical, Social, and Economic Research (ISSER) (1997). *The State of the Ghanaian Economy in 1996* (University of Ghana, Legon).

Institute of Statistical, Social, and Economic Research (ISSER) (1998). *The State of the Ghanaian Economy in 1997* (University of Ghana, Legon).

Jaffee, S. (1993). "Kenya's Horticultural Export Marketing: A Transaction Cost Perspective," in Abbott, J. (Ed.), *Agricultural and Food Marketing in Developing Countries: Selected Readings* (C.A.B. International, Wallingford, United Kingdom), pp. 388-403.

Jebuni, C.D., Oduro, A., Asante, Y., and Tsikata, G.K. (1992). *Diversifying Exports: Supply Response of Non-Traditional Exports to Measures Under the ERP.* ODI Research Report (Overseas Development Institute and University of Ghana, London and Ghana).

Johanson, J. and Mattsson, L.-G. (1988). "Internationalization in Industrial Systems—A Network Approach," in Hood, N. and Vahlne, J.E. (Eds.), *Strategies in Global Competition* (Wiley, London), pp. 287-314.

Johanson, J. and Vahlne, J. (1977). "The Internationalization Process of the Firm—A Model of Knowledge Development and Increasing Foreign Market Commitments," *Journal of International Business Studies,* Vol. 8, No. 1, pp. 23-32.

Johanson, J. and Wiedersheim-Paul, F. (1975). "The Internationalization of the Firm—Four Swedish Case Studies," *The Journal of Management Studies*, Vol. 12, No. 3, pp. 305-322.

Johansson, J.K. and Nonaka, I. (1987). "Market Research the Japanese Way," *Harvard Business Review,* Vol. 65, No. 3, pp. 16-22.

Katsikeas, C.S. and Morgan, R.E. (1994). "Differences in Perceptions of Exporting Problems Based on Firm Size and Export Market Experience," *European Journal of Marketing,* Vol. 28, No. 5, pp. 16-34.

Kaynak, E. and Hudanah, B.I. (1987). "Operationalizing the Relationship Between Marketing and Economic Development: Some Insights from Less Developed Countries," *European Journal of Marketing*, Vol. 21, No. 1, pp. 48-65.

Keegan, W.J. (1974). "Multinational Scanning: A Study of the Information Source Utilized by Headquarters Executives in Multinational Companies," *Administrative Science Quarterly*, Vol. 19, No. 4, pp. 411-421.

Keegan, W.J. (1989). *Global Marketing Management,* Fourth Edition (Prentice-Hall International Inc., Englewood Cliffs, New Jersey).

Keesing, D.B. and Lall, S. (1991). "Marketing Manufactured Exports from Developing Countries: Learning Sequences and Public Support," in Helleiner, G. (Ed.), *Trade Policy: Industrialisation and Development: New Perspectives* (Clarendon Press, Oxford).

Kinsey, J. (1988). *Marketing in Developing Countries* (Macmillan Education Ltd., London).

Kotabe, M. and Czinkota, M.R. (1992). "State Government Promotion of Manufacturing Exports: A Gap Analysis," *Journal of International Business Studies,* Vol. 23, No. 4, pp. 637-658.

Kuada, J. (1993). "Knowledge Acquisition and the Internationalization Process of Firms: Some Reflections on the Contemporary Literature," *Working Paper Series,* No. 2 (International Business Economics, Aalborg University, Aalborg, Denmark), pp. 1-23.

Kuada, J. (1994). *Managerial Behaviour in Ghana and Kenya: A Cultural Perspective* (Aalborg University Press, Aalborg, Denmark).

Kuada, J. and Sørensen, O.J. (1995). "Structural Adjustment and the Internationalization of Ghanaian Companies." Paper presented at the Fifth International Conference on Marketing and Development, Beijing, June 22-25.

Kuada, J. and Sørensen, O.J. (1997). "Planning-Oriented vs. Action-Based Approach to the Internationalization of Firms," *Working Paper Series,* No. 22 (Center for International Studies, Aalborg University, Aalborg, Denmark).

Lall, S. (1991). "Marketing Barriers Facing Developing Country Manufactured Exporters: A Conceptual Note," *The Journal of Development Studies,* Vol. 27, No. 4, pp. 137-150.

Lall, S. and Wignaraja, G. (1996). "Skills and Capabilities: Ghana's Industrial Competitiveness," *Development Studies Working Papers,* No. 92 (University of Oxford, Oxford), pp. 1-33.

Lamming, R. (1993). *Beyond Partnership: Strategies for Innovation and Lean Supply* (Prentice-Hall, London).

Langfield-Smith, K. (1992). "Exploring the Need for a Shared Cognitive Map," *Journal of Management Studies,* Vol. 29, No. 3, pp. 349-366.

Lawrence, P.R. and Lorsch, J.W. (1967). *Organization and Environment* (Harvard Graduate School of Business, Cambridge, Massachusetts).

Leonard, D.K. (1987). "The Political Realities of African Management," *World Development,* Vol. 15, No. 7, pp. 899-910.

Leonidou, C.L. and Katsikeas, C.S. (1996). "The Export Development Process: An Intergrative Review of Empirical Models," *Journal of International Business Studies,* Vol. 27, No. 3, pp. 517-551.

Lessem, R. (1989). *Global Management Principles* (Prentice-Hall International, Inc., Hertfordshire, United Kingdom).

Levy, B. (1994). "Technical and Marketing Support Systems for Successful Small- and Medium-Size Enterprises in Four Countries." Policy Research Working Paper No. 1400 (World Bank, Washington, DC).

Lim, J.-S., Sharkey, W.S., and Kim, K.I. (1996). "Competitive Environmental Scanning and Export Involvement: An Initial Enquiry," *International Marketing Review,* Vol. 13, No. 1, pp. 65-80.

Loxley, J. (1988). *Ghana: Economic Crisis and the Long Road to Recovery* (The North-South Institute, Ottawa, Ontario, Canada).

March, J.G. and Olsen, J.P. (1976). *Ambiguity and Choice in Organizations* (Universitetsforlaget, Bergen, Norway).

Marsden, K. (1990). "African Entrepreneurs: Pioneers of Development," Discussion Paper No. 9 (International Finance Corporation, Washington, DC).

Mayer, C.S. (1978). "Lesson from Multinational Marketing Research," *Business Horizons,* Vol. 21, No. 4, pp. 7-13.

McAuley, A. (1993). "The Perceived Usefulness of Export Information Sources," *European Journal of Marketing,* Vol. 27, No. 10, pp. 52-64.

Meyerson, D. and Martin, J. (1987). "Cultural Change: An Integration of Different Views," *Journal of Management Studies,* Vol. 24, No. 6, pp. 623-647.

Michalet, C.-A. (1991). "Strategic Partnerships and the Changing Internationalization Process," in Mytelka, L.K. (Ed.), *Strategic Partnerships: States, Firms and International Competition* (Pinter Publishers, London), pp. 34-49.

Miesenbock, K.J. (1988). "Small Business and Exporting: A Literature Review," *International Small Business Journal,* Vol. 6, No. 2, pp. 42-61.

Mittendorf, H.J. (1982). "Topics for Studies on Agricultural and Food Marketing in Developing Countries," *Quarterly Journal of International Agriculture,* Vol. 21, No. 2, pp. 139-154.

Montgomery, J.D. (1987). "Probing Managerial Behavior: Images and Reality in Southern Africa," *World Development,* Vol. 15, No. 7, pp. 911-929.

Morgan, R.M. and Hunt, S.D. (1994). "The Commitment-Trust Theory of Relationship Marketing," *Journal of Marketing,* Vol. 58, No. 3, pp. 21-37.

Moss, C. (1979). "Industrial Salesmen As a Source of Marketing Intelligence," *European Journal of Marketing,* Vol. 13, No. 3, pp. 94-102.

Nohria, N. (1992). "Is a Network Perspective a Useful Way of Studying Organizations?" in Nohria, N. and Eccles, R.G. (Eds.), *Networks and Organizations: Structure, Form, and Action* (Harvard Business School Press, Boston), pp. 1-2.

Nugent, P. (1995). *Big Men, Small Boys and Politics in Ghana: Power Ideology and the Burden of History* (Pinter Publishers, London and New York).

Oduro, A.D. (1994). "The Direction of Ghana's Export Trade in the Nineteen Eighties," *African Journal of Economic Policy,* Vol. 1, No. 1, pp. 125-140.

O'Farrell, P.N. and Wood, P.A. (1994). "International Market Selection by Business Service Firms: Key Conceptual and Methodological Issues," *International Business Review,* Vol. 3, No. 3, pp. 243-261.

Olsen, E.J., Biswas, A., and Kacker, M. (1992). "The Changing European Market: Strategies for Companies from Developing Nations," *Journal of Euromarketing,* Vol. 2, No. 1, pp. 99-115.

Ouchi, W.G. (1980). "Markets, Bureaucracies and Clans," *Administrative Science Quarterly,* Vol. 25, No. 4, pp. 129-141.

Pascale, R.T. (1984). "Perspectives on Strategy: The Real Story Behind Honda's Success," *California Management Review,* Vol. 26, No. 3, pp. 47-72.

Pedler, M., Burgoyne, J., and Boydell, T. (1991). *The Learning Company: A Strategy for Sustainable Development* (McGraw-Hill, London).

Permut, S.E. (1977). "The European View of Marketing Research," *Columbia Journal of World Business,* Vol. 12, No. 3, pp. 94-104.

Porter, M.E. (1986). "Changing Pattern of International Competition," *California Management Review,* Vol. XXVII, No. 2 (Winter), pp. 9-38.

Porter, M.E. (1990). *The Competitive Advantage of Nations* (Macmillan Press, London).

Porter, M.E. (1994). "The Role of Location in Competition," *Journal of the Economics of Business,* Vol. 1, No. 1, pp. 35-39.

Powell, W. (1991). "Neither Market nor Hierarchy: Network Forms of Organization," in Thompson, G., Frances, G., Levacic, R.L., and Mitchell, J. (Eds.), *Markets, Hierarchies and Networks* (Sage Publications, London), pp. 265-276.

Prahalad, C.K. and Hamel, G. (1990). "The Core Competence of the Corporation," *Harvard Business Review,* Vol. 68, No. 3, pp. 79-91.

Reed, M. (1965). *Marketing in Economic Development* (Michigan State University, East Lansing, Michigan).

Reusse, E. (1976). "Economic and Market Aspects of Post-Harvest Systems in Small Farmer Economics," *Monthly Bulletin of Agricultural Economics and Statistics,* Vol. 25, No. 9, pp. 1-7.

Rhee, Y.W. and Belot, T. (1990). "Export Catalysts in Low-Income Countries: A Review of Eleven Success Stories," *World Bank Discussion Paper,* No. 72 (World Bank, Washington, DC).

Root, F.R. (1987). *Entry Strategies for International Markets* (Lexington Books, Lexington, Massachusetts).

Sackmann, S.A. (1992). "Culture and Subcultures: An Analysis of Organizational Knowledge," *Administrative Science Quarterly,* Vol. 37, No. 1, pp. 140-161.

Schein, H.E. (1971). "The Individual, the Organization, and the Career: A Conceptual Scheme," *Journal of Applied Behavioral Science,* Vol. 7, No. 2, pp. 401-416.

Schlegelmilch, B.B. (1986). "Controlling Country-Specific and Industry-Specific Influences on Export Behaviour," *European Journal of Marketing,* Vol. 20, No. 2, pp. 54-71.

Schmitz, H. and Musyck B. (1994). "Industrial Districts in Europe: Policy Lessons for Developing Countries?" *World Development,* Vol. 22, No. 6, pp. 889-910.

Senge, P. (1990). *The Fifth Discipline: The Art and Practice of the Learning Organization, Country Business* (Doubleday, Currency, New York).

Seringhaus, R.F.H. and Botschen G. (1991). "Cross-National Comparison of Export Promotion Services: The Views of Canadian and Austrian Companies," *Journal of International Business Studies,* Vol. 22, No. 1, pp. 115-133.

Sharkey, T.W., Lim, J.S., and Kim, K.L. (1989). "Export Development and Perceived Export Barriers: An Empirical Analysis of Small Firms," *Management International Review,* Vol. 29, No. 2, pp. 33-41.

Simpson, C.L. and Kujawa, D. (1974). "The Export Decision Process: An Empirical Enquiry," *Journal of International Business Studies,* Vol. 5, No. 2, pp. 107-117.

Sørensen, O.J. (1991). "The Internationalization of Enterprises: Mechanical Evolution or Strategic Development, in Veggeland, N. (Ed.), *The Small-Sized Company* (in Danish only) (NordRefo, Academic Press, Copenhagen), pp. 53-74.

Sørensen, O.J. (1994a). "Approaches to Analyzing International Industries," *Study Material Series,* No. 5 (Centre for International Studies, Aalborg University, Aalborg, Denmark), pp. 1-28.

Sørensen, O.J. (1994b). "Government-Business Relations: Towards a Partnership Model," *Working Paper Series,* No. 9 (Centre for International Studies, Aalborg University, Aalborg, Denmark), pp. 1-28.

Sørensen, O.J. (1995). "The Network Theory: An Introduction to Its Conceptual World," *Study Material Series,* No. 8 (Centre for International Studies, Aalborg University, Aalborg, Denmark), pp. 1-18.

Sørensen, O.J. (1996a). "Alternative Ways of Choosing International Market Entry Modes," *Study Materials Series,* No. 9 (Centre for International Studies, Aalborg University, Aalborg, Denmark), pp. 1-9.

Sørensen O.J. (1996b). Global Organization of Production. Lecture notes. (Centre for International Studies, Aalborg University, Aalborg, Denmark).

Sørensen, O.J. and Christensen, P. (1993). "Spændingsfelter Mellem Regionale Erhvervsudvikling og International Konkurrence," in Lorentzen, A., Rieper, O., and Svensson, B. (Eds.), *Teknologiudvilkling og Regional Forandring* (Amternes og Kommunernes Forskningsinstitut, Copenhagen), pp. 113-144.

Sørensen, O.J. and Kuada, J. (1997). "Institutional Context of Ghanaian Firms and Cross-National Inter-Firm Relations." Paper presented at Workshop on Business Systems in the South, Copenhagen School of Business, Copenhagen, January 22-24.

Sørensen, O.J. and Kuada, J. (1998a). "Approaches to the Integration of Ghanaian Companies into the Global Economy: The Case of Non-Traditional Products," *Working Paper Series,* No. 30 (Centre for International Studies, Aalborg University, Aalborg, Denmark), pp. 1-21.

Sørensen, O.J. and Kuada, J. (1998b). "International Strategic Alliance in Business Development: The Case of Ghana," *Working Paper Series,* No. 39 (Centre for International Studies, Aalborg University, Aalborg, Denmark), pp. 1-24.

Sørensen, O.J. and Nedergaard, A. (1993). "Management Decision Making in an International Context: The Case of Intuition and Action Learning," *Working*

Paper Series, No. 7 (Centre for International Studies, Aalborg University, Aalborg, Denmark), pp. 1-15.

Strandskov, J. (1987). *Hvor Internationale er Danske Virksomheder?* (Samfundslitteratur, Copenhagen).

Strandskov, J. (1995). *Internationalisering af Virksomheder* (Nyere Teoretiske Perspektiver, Handelshøjskolens Forlag, Copenhagen).

Sullivan, D. and Bauerschmidt, A. (1988). "Common Factors Underlying Incentive to Export: Studies in the European Forest Products Industry," *European Journal of Marketing,* Vol. 22, No. 10, pp. 41-55.

Tetteh, D.O. (1996). "Institutional Support for Non-Traditional Exports in Ghana." MBA thesis. (University of Ghana, School of Administration, Legon, Ghana).

Thomas, M.J. and Araujo, L. (1985). "Theories of Export Behaviour: A Critical Analysis," *European Journal of Marketing,* Vol. 19, No. 2, pp. 42-52.

Toye, J. (1990). "Ghana's Economic Reforms (1983-1987): Origins, Achievements and Limitations." A paper presented in Seminar on Structural Adjustment Programmes, Copenhagen, Denmark.

Toye, J. (1994). "Structural Adjustment: Context, Assumptions, Origin and Diversity," *Poverty and Development,* No. 11. (Ministry of Foreign Affairs, the Development Cooperation Information Department, The Hague), pp. 24-29.

Toyne, B. and Walters, P.G.P. (1989). *Global Marketing Management: A Strategic Perspective* (Allyn and Bacon, Needham Heights, Massachusetts).

Tsikata, G.K. and Amuzu, G.K. (1993). "Fiscal Development," in Nyanteng, V.K. (Ed.), *Policies and Options for Ghanaian Economic Development* (University of Ghana, The Institute of Statistical, Social and Economic Research, Legon, Ghana), pp. 1-24.

Turnbull, P.W. (1987). "A Challenge to the Stages Theory of the Internationalization Process," in Rosson, P.J. and Reed, S.D. (Eds.), *Managing Export Entry and Expansion* (Praeger, New York), pp. 21-40.

Varadarajan, R.P. (1984). "Marketing in Developing Countries: The New Frontier," *Long Range Planning,* Vol. 17, No. 6, pp. 118-126.

Vernon, R. (1966). "International Investment and International Trade in the Product Cycle," *Quarterly Journal of Economics,* Vol. 80, No. 2, pp. 190-207.

Vernon-Wortzel, H., Wortzel, L.H., and Deng, S. (1988). "Do Neophyte Exporters Understand Importers?" *Columbia Journal of World Business,* Vol. 23, No. 4, pp. 49-56.

Weick, K.E. (1979). "Cognitive Processes in Organizations," in Staw, B.M. (Ed.), *Research in Organizational Behavior* (JAI Press, Greenwich, Connecticut), pp. 41-74.

Welch, L.S. and Wiedersheim-Paul, F. (1980). "Initial Exports—A Marketing Failure," *Journal of Management Studies,* Vol. 17, No. 3, pp. 333-344.

Welch, L.S. and Luostarinen, R. (1988). "Internationalization: Evolution of a Concept," *Journal of General Management*, Vol. 14, No. 2, pp. 34-55.

Welch, L.S. and Luostarinen, R. (1993). "Inward-outward Connections in Internationalization," *Journal of International Marketing*, Vol. 1, No. 1, pp. 44-56.

Whitley, R. (1990). "Eastern Asian Enterprise Structures and the Comparative Analysis of Forms of Business Organizations," *Organization Studies,* Vol. 11, No. 1, pp. 47-54.

Whitley, R. (1991). "The Social Construction of Business Systems in East Asia," *Organization Studies*, Vol. 12, No. 1, pp. 1-28.

Whitley, R. (1992). *Business Systems in East Asia: Firms, Markets and Societies* (Sage Publications, London).

Whitley, R. (Ed.) (1994). *European Business Systems: Firms and Markets in Their National Context* (Sage Publications, London).

Wiedersheim-Paul, F., Olson, H.C., and Welch, L.S. (1978). "Pre-export and Activity: The First Step in Internationalization," *Journal of International Business Studies,* Vol. 9, No. 1, pp. 47-58.

Wilkins, A.L. and Ouchi, W.G. (1983). "Efficient Cultures: Exploring the Relationship Between Culture and Organizational Performance," *Administrative Science Quarterly,* Vol. 28, No. 3, pp. 468-481.

Williamson, O.E. (1975). *Markets and Hierarchies* (The Free Press, New York).

Williamson, O.E. (1979). "Transaction-Cost Economics: The Governance of Contractual Relations," *Journal of Law and Economics*, Vol. 22, No. 2, pp. 233-261.

Williamson, O.E. (1981). "The Economics of Organization: The Transaction Cost Approach," *American Journal of Sociology*, Vol. 87, No. 3, pp. 548-577.

World Bank (1995). "Supply and Demand for Finance of Small Enterprises in Ghana," *World Bank Discussion Papers,* No. 251 (World Bank, Washington, DC).

Wortzel, L.H. and Vernon-Wortzel, H. (1981). "Export Marketing Strategies for NIC and LDC-Based Firms," *Columbia Journal of World Business* (Spring), Vol. 16, No. 2, pp. 51-66.

Young, S., Hamill, J., Wheeler, C., and Davis, R.J. (1989). *International Market Entry and Development* (Harvester Wheatsheaf, London).

Zeldenrust-Noordanus, M. (1976). "Why, When and How Cross-Cultural Behaviour Studies," *Proceedings from Seminar on International Marketing Research—Does It Provide What the User Needs?* (ESOMAR, Amsterdam), pp. 181-194.

Index

Williamson, O. E., 19, 189
Wood, P. A., 36, 45
Wood products, 107
Woody Limited, 115, 123, 124
World Bank, 94, 100, 152
Worldviews, 10-11
Wortzel, L. H., 2, 77, 78

Yams, 106, 116
Young, S., 57, 61

Zimbabwe, 49

Order Your Own Copy of
This Important Book for Your Personal Library!

INTERNATIONALIZATION OF COMPANIES
FROM DEVELOPING COUNTRIES

_____ in hardbound at $79.95 (ISBN: 0-7890-0721-5)

_____ in softbound at $39.95 (ISBN: 0-7890-1079-8)

COST OF BOOKS_____

OUTSIDE USA/CANADA/
MEXICO: ADD 20%_____

POSTAGE & HANDLING_____
*(US: $3.00 for first book & $1.25
for each additional book)
Outside US: $4.75 for first book
& $1.75 for each additional book)*

SUBTOTAL_____

IN CANADA: ADD 7% GST_____

STATE TAX_____
*(NY, OH & MN residents, please
add appropriate local sales tax)*

FINAL TOTAL_____
*(If paying in Canadian funds,
convert using the current
exchange rate. UNESCO
coupons welcome.)*

☐ **BILL ME LATER:** ($5 service charge will be added)
(Bill-me option is good on US/Canada/Mexico orders only;
not good to jobbers, wholesalers, or subscription agencies.)

☐ Check here if billing address is different from
shipping address and attach purchase order and
billing address information.

Signature _____

☐ **PAYMENT ENCLOSED: $** _____

☐ **PLEASE CHARGE TO MY CREDIT CARD.**

☐ Visa   ☐ MasterCard   ☐ AmEx   ☐ Discover
☐ Diner's Club

Account # _____

Exp. Date _____

Signature _____

Prices in US dollars and subject to change without notice.

NAME _____

INSTITUTION _____

ADDRESS _____

CITY _____

STATE/ZIP _____

COUNTRY _____ COUNTY (NY residents only) _____

TEL _____ FAX _____

E-MAIL_____

May we use your e-mail address for confirmations and other types of information? ☐ Yes   ☐ No

Order From Your Local Bookstore or Directly From
The Haworth Press, Inc.
10 Alice Street, Binghamton, New York 13904-1580 • USA
TELEPHONE: 1-800-HAWORTH (1-800-429-6784) / Outside US/Canada: (607) 722-5857
FAX: 1-800-895-0582 / Outside US/Canada: (607) 772-6362
E-mail: getinfo@haworthpressinc.com
PLEASE PHOTOCOPY THIS FORM FOR YOUR PERSONAL USE.

BOF96